Home Is Where the Wine Is

Laurie Perry

Health Communications, Inc.
Deerfield Beach, Florida

www.hcibooks.com

Disclaimer: The events described in this book are true as I remember them, best as I could what with being covered in cat hair and three minutes from directing traffic in my nightgown. Some names and details have been changed.

Library of Congress Cataloging-in-Publication Data

Perry, Laurie.
    Home is where the wine is: making the most of what you've got one stitch (and cocktail!) at a time / Laurie Perry.
        p. cm.
    ISBN-13: 978-0-7573-1368-4
    ISBN-10: 0-7573-1368-X
    1. Conduct of life—Humor.   2. Drinking of alcoholic beverages—Humor.
    3. Dating (Social customs)—Humor.   4. Knitting—Humor.   5. Perry, Laurie.
    I. Title.
    PN6231.C6142P43 2010
    818'.5402—dc22

                                                                                2009048175

Publisher: Health Communications, Inc.
            3201 S.W. 15th Street
            Deerfield Beach, FL 33442-8190

Cover design by Andrea Perrine Brower
Interior design and formatting by Lawna Patterson Oldfield

For all the
crazy cat
ladies

Contents

January 1:
Resolutions

Old Year

December 31, 9 p.m.
La Habra, California
Sunny Lake Retirement Community

It's New Year's Eve. Once again I have the disturbing feeling I should be somewhere more fun and exciting, wearing a funny hat and age-inappropriate glitter while drunkenly sloshing something on my fancy dress.

Instead I am wearing pajamas and my glasses, and I am locked in the bathroom at my grandmother's house in Orange County. We just watched the West Hollywood Gay Men's Chorus on TV, and she turned to ask me if I thought being gay was a requirement to join the chorus or if it was just a learning opportunity.

I am drinking wine out of a Styrofoam cup with my name penned on it. Grandma wrote my name on the cup so I would remember which one was mine. This is my family's version of going green.

Tonight, for the first time ever, I realized that my five-year plan includes turning FORTY YEARS OLD. My grandmother, well into her eighties, is still drinking bourbon and making jokes, but for some reason I am more terrified of one day being forty than of one day being eighty.

Also, since I am being honest, instead of really wanting to be at a cool party, I secretly just miss my cats who are probably puking on my new bathroom rug, unaware that we are on the cusp of a new year, a new start, a brand-new, freshly unopened calendar whose 365 days could hold unending surprise. I need to make some changes. I have to get my life together. I should make some resolutions. I should refill this Styrofoam cup.

The Morning After

After eating the required spoonful of black-eyed peas (for good luck!) and eating my way out of a jeans size at breakfast, I left Grandma's house and drove back to my own little corner of the world. My life, contained in 800 square feet of rented bliss in the San Fernando Valley. When I moved in, the landlord made me sign a disclaimer saying I wouldn't eat the paint or gnaw on the door frames, since the house was so old it was practically held together by lead-based paint from years gone by.

When I started my New Year's resolutions, there was no one in the house except for me and the cats—and a surprisingly large amount of champagne in little single-person sizes, which

I couldn't help buying everywhere I saw them on sale until I had the equivalent of a miniature champagne farm in my cupboard. I opened a fresh notebook and began to ponder this new year, this new opportunity to become the person I'd always wanted to be:

New Year's Resolutions (first draft)
Start drinking champagne at noon
Clean the cat box

I am about to turn the corner from "midthirties" to "mid-to-wrinkled thirties," and my life has settled into a rhythm that is certainly less dramatic and grief-encompassing than the past few years, but not nearly exciting enough to send out happy Christmas letters written in the third person, annoying all my friends and family about the minutia of my life.

New Year's resolutions feel powerful, like they have the transformative mojo to add purpose and excitement to your life and make over your wardrobe and your love life, and change your entire path. I want those resolutions; I want the list that will advance me ever nearer bliss and fulfillment—and forty.

But I am a realist; I can't see myself running off and joining an ashram and shaving my head to find enlightenment. I just paid my hairdresser to give me shiny New Year highlights, and I have yet to find an ashram that takes cats.

x

New Year's Resolutions (second draft)
- *Stop reading books about other people that make me feel jealous and want to stab them with a fork*
- *Become a better person*
- *Clean the cat box*

It is an attainable list, especially with "become a better person" so loosely defined.

What I need is a purpose. An overarching life goal. And a pool boy. I want to change my life; I want happiness—whatever that is.

There Is Nothing Wrong with Me, Still I Search

Some of my resolutions, such as "become a better person," are works in progress and not immediately achievable, while others, such as "try five new things (not all of them food items)," "clean the cat box every day," and "send at least two birthday cards on time" seem doable. But in terms of whole-life changes, there is no single resolution I can make, so my final list is fairly brief:

1. *Explore New Paths to Enlightenment.*
2. *Take an Adventurous Trip.*
3. *Knit Something That Isn't Square.*
4. *Go on a Real, Live Date (Versus a Pretend One with Jason Bourne-Anderson Cooper/George Clooney).*
5. *Grow a Garden.*

6. *Deal with My Issues*
7. *Try Something New (and Not Just a New Food)*
8. *Do Some Form of Exercise Other than Knitting*

I read my list over the phone to my friend Drew, who lives in Houston. Talking to my long-distance friends and family is now much cheaper than therapy since the advent of the Fave-5s cell phone plan. Once I read the list out loud, it doesn't sound like much.

"At this point in my life I feel like I should have accomplished more," I tell Drew.

"But you wrote a book," he says.

"True, but the first word in the title is *Drunk*," I said. "It's not exactly going to win a Pulitzer anytime soon. You think there's money with a Pulitzer? And now I get letters from guys in prison who tell me they like cats and girls who write books with *Drunk* in the title. They're a very loyal audience."

"So what is it you think you should have accomplished by now?"

"I don't know . . . I'm not sure where I go from here. I don't want to get married again. I think I'm still paying off my divorce. I don't think I'm ready for kids. That in itself makes me morally suspect to virtually everyone I know."

"Well," he said, "you could be gay. That would give you a way to stay unmarried, and you'd only have to consider adopting, although you'd have to go antiquing at least once."

I laugh out loud. Drew always makes me laugh.

"While that certainly is enticing, the only thing I do know for sure is that I'm not gay." I sigh. "It's a shame, really. If I met someone my own size it would be like an instant wardrobe expansion."

"Are you depressed?" he asked.

"Maybe. Mostly I'm just funky. Shouldn't I be more . . . *finished* by now?"

"Finished?" asked Drew. "Like dead?"

"No, like completed and assured! I should own a home, drive a car with at least one air bag, and have goals." Now I am really on a roll. My unfinishedness has become more apparent over the past year, as my friends get more grown-up and responsible and I seem to go in the other direction.

"I mean real goals. Everyone I know except you is out having children or actively looking for someone to mate with. Or they have thriving careers and feel deeply connected to their Pilates class. I should have a purpose to my life, a connection with someone; instead I can't even commit to a hair color. I feel like I am a terrible adult—that I should be more enlightened. And one day I am going to be forty. I am going to turn forty . . . Eventually."

We talked a while longer and made jokes about my unfinishedness. And even though I knew the messy feeling inside me was self-indulgent—I'm healthy and I have a good life—it was there. But being grateful for what I've accomplished doesn't make me want less out of life; it makes we want to live more. I have no idea what the future holds. It's refreshing and also unsettling, and anything could happen.

So that is how I started off the year, by deciding to take myself on as an art project. I smoothed out the notebook paper list and placed my resolutions on my bathroom mirror.

"Anything can happen," I told myself.

When in Doubt, Buy a Glue Stick

Drew comes to visit at least once a year. We usually spend our time shopping at Bloomingdales, eating at restaurants I never go to on my own, and looking for celebrities in the Whole Foods Market in the valley. Our visits always begin with me picking him up at the airport—sometimes I am even on time— and then we go immediately to In-N-Out Burger and order cheeseburgers and take them back to my house and eat this feast with copious amounts of wine and catching-up talk.

There is no reason to think we would deviate from our normal get-togethers, except this time Drew is arriving during my apex of growthiness.

We drive through the In-N-Out Burger nearest my house, haul his luggage and our double-doubles back to my house, eat and drink and be merry, and then he asks what's on the schedule for the night.

"We're going to make vision boards," I said.

"Is *vision board* a code word for 'go to the private sale at Bloomies'?" he asked.

"A vision board is this supposedly very valuable tool in which you focus all your desires for your perfect life and cut pictures out of magazines and glue them to poster board," I am rather full of myself and my double-double by now. "And so I have a big stack of magazines and two enormous pieces of foam core and glue sticks. I even bought you your own pair of scissors because I didn't want to use my knitting scissors on magazines. So eat up, and then we will carefully and with great attention to detail make vision boards, and then I can quit my job and move to the beach—and I will be taller!"

"I see," said Drew. "And where did you hear about this poster-board vision?"

"It's from *Oprah*. Well, it was a segment they had on *Oprah* and . . . don't laugh at me. Oprah is a very powerful person." I said.

"Do you think Oprah has a vision board?" asked Drew.

"What do you think Oprah would have on her vision board? Do you think you ever reach a place where you say, 'Okay! That's it! I have achieved everything and I am complete!' Do you think that happens?" I asked. Earnestly. Perhaps a little tightly wound.

"I think that happens when you croak," he said.

So we finished our gourmet meal and I handed him a glue stick and a stack of magazines, and because he is a good friend— and also because this is not even the tip of the crazy iceberg when it comes to things I have done around him—we sat there pleasantly drinking wine and pasting cutouts of cute armchairs and outfits and houses on our foam boards.

"How do we know if it's working?" I asked.

"I think I'm getting high from the glue stick," said Drew.

Self-help, knitting, even pasting pictures on a poster board—why not? I'll try it all.

Comfortably full on hamburgers, fries, and pinot grigio, I watched my dear friend try to paste a picture of an Hermès belt next to a cutout of a baby-blue convertible. One of my cats brushed by as I rubbed my glue stick on the back of a clipping, and she walked away with a picture of a gorgeous turquoise beach glued to her furry tail. Perfect moments are so small you sometimes only remember them from the food you ate or the fumes from the glue, but my perfect moment now sits memorialized in my bedroom, all the little pictures of my ideal future cut and pasted onto poster board, some with a little tuft of soft calico fur.

Does Meditation Burn Calories?

The first time I tried to officially meditate was on a Sunday morning. There's a fabulous new-agey church here in Los Angeles that I go to sometimes. But it's also a phenomenally popular place, which means you have to get there early to get a parking spot. Nothing makes you madder than trying to get all filled up with love and inspiration and being unable to do so because there is no parking. In fact, that has quite the opposite effect.

Before the service starts, there's a thirty-minute group

meditation period. You don't have to participate, you can just attend the service, but since I drove in early one Sunday for a coveted parking space, I also arrived in time for meditation, and that seemed lucky. Maybe group meditation is the way to go, I thought. With all the collective power of practiced meditators in the room, perhaps I could finally dip into the mystic!

I took a seat in the back and tried to sit as comfortably as possible. I put my handbag away, took off my jacket, and stretched my neck a little in preparation for thirty minutes of stillness and peace.

A lanky guitar player took the stage, and a woman with a soothing, melodic voice began to speak. I closed my eyes and the music began to slow, and the woman speaker became silent, and then the music stopped completely and the lights were all the way dim and the room was . . . *not silent at all*. A cough here. A sneeze there. Someone to the left cleared his throat. The room was empty of words but filled with combined exhalations, coughs, sneezes, shuffles, and sighs. It was a room overflowing with all the sounds of a wordless population. Reflexively, I opened my eyes and began counting people. I began to think of all these people, nearly 170 of them, just inhaling and exhaling. Deeply. Over and over again, recycling the air. Then someone right in front of me sneezed, loudly, wetly. Another cough, this time closer to the front. I squirmed in my seat. Group meditation was not working. Group meditation was making me want an antibacterial wet wipe *immediately*.

It was an awkward and germaphobic-inducing thirty minutes. When the melodic voice of the speaker and the soft strings of guitar began again toward the end, I jumped out of my seat and ran to the ladies' room to vigorously wash my hands.

I haven't been back to group meditation since that one Sunday. I just can't meditate in a confined space with other people sneezing and coughing and breathing in and out all the time with nothing to distract me from the mass exhalation of germs. I don't think my response is so unusual. It's probably quite sensible, actually, especially during the cold and flu season.

But I didn't give up on meditation. After my germ-filled venture into group breathing, I bought a few books on meditation techniques I could try in the privacy of my own home. One thick book has all sorts of different practices, and some even have props. The first one I tried seemed like a good idea—a candle meditation. You just look at the flame and think about the flame, which seemed infinitely preferable to emptying the mind and thinking of nothing at all.

The candle I chose was plain beeswax but set into a beautiful little glass votive holder. I lit the wick and sat it on the coffee table and stared at it. *This might work,* I thought, and then I began to concentrate on the flame. The lovely, warm flame.

My cat Frankie took a great interest in this new activity. She has never seen me stare at a candle on the coffee table. I don't light candles much, because I am afraid the cats will get too close, or knock them over, or we'll have an earthquake and a gas explosion will happen because I was using candles for my yuppie attempt at ambience. Some people say I worry too much, but I'm just a planner, that's all.

Frankie is especially interested in all things that sit on the coffee table because sometimes they might be edible, like tortilla chips (her favorite), and sometimes there are cups left unattended for just two seconds and that is a perfect amount of time to take a nice, refreshing drink and leave a little fur in the glass. You cannot leave anything uncovered or unguarded around her; she thinks all humans exist solely to bring her food and drinks, and the world is a delightful place to explore with her kitty mouth.

As I focused on my candle meditation, Frankie jumped onto the coffee table and moved right up to the candle. I tried to shoo her away—peaceful, Zenlike shooing—but the pretty glass votive holder is shaped a lot like a drinking glass. Frankie *loves* drinking out of a glass, because sometimes there are ice cubes. Frankie loves ice cubes. I see her coming back for round two, and I know she's thinking some cat version of *ice cube, ice cube, must have ice cube,* and she jumps back on the coffee table, this time just an inch away from the flame, and now I'm starting to worry that she'll singe her fur or her long whiskers will catch fire and that might require a trip to the vet and she hates riding in the car and yelps the whole way there and back and I am starting to get anxious, which is not part of the meditation. I vow not to be irritated at the cat, I vow not to abandon meditation, so I take my beeswax candle and go into the bedroom *alone* and close the door. I put the candle on the nightstand, sit on the floor, and try to focus on it. And that is when the mauling begins.

My cats ignore me for most of my day. They are sometimes interested in me if I'm bringing them food, but usually I am just an annoyance who moves too much at night when they are finally comfortable and warm in the bed. If it is a hot night, they don't bother with me at all; they just sit in their little kitty beds and sleep. The cats only interrupt their sleeping to eat whatever I bring them, and then they poop. And poop some more. I am a mere cog in the poop-scooping wheel of their kitty lives.

But if you close the door—any door—to any room in the house, suddenly they are all insane with desire to enter the forbidden space. They wail for help, they cry, they carry on like wild beasts. They cannot be on the other side of the door! Whatever is inside the closed room must be theirs! Then and only then they come together as a team, one hitting up against the door, one clawing at it from above, and one with a paw stuck underneath to signal, "In case you didn't know, we're out here! Alone! You forgot us!"

And sometimes I know that what they are really saying is that they were left out and are pissed off and might puke in my handbag in the middle of the night if I don't let them in RIGHT NOW.

So the bedroom door is assaulted by three angry felines with hairy fists of rage. It is not really the peaceful, calm vibration I had hoped to achieve with candle meditation. One cat is clawing at the carpet below the door while another hurls his sixteen-pound body against it. I blow out the candle, open the door, and the cats run into the bedroom, look everything over, and upon seeing that nothing is new or edible in the room, they immediately return to ignoring me. Candle meditation is officially over. Check.

I flipped through the meditation technique book and found one that I could do outdoors alone called "walking practice," where you walk slowly and carefully and focus entirely on your movements. I read the instructions twice and went into my cat-less backyard to begin my walk for inner peace. My next-door neighbors were standing in their driveway talking and looking through the bamboo fencing, so I had to go behind the hedge to practice my walking meditation without being seen. No one wants to be known as the crazy lady with all the cats who walks in slow motion in her own backyard.

I found a spot in the grass hidden from my neighbors' view, and I was doing pretty well at first—slowly lifting my foot, breathing in and out, slowly lowering my foot—until I realized I was standing in an anthill and my left Ugg boot was being rapidly conquered by tiny black insects. I gave a little shout and hopped off, trying to shake the ants off my boots.

"You okay back there?" asked my neighbor. He poked his head above the fence.

"I'm fine," I said. "Ants." I pointed to my shoes.

"You should get some rubber boots for gardening if you're going to be back by the shrubs," he said. "Sometimes there's rats way back in the ivy."

With that I fled indoors, away from the wild natural world and back to the persnickety domesticated housecat world. Where there is wine. And tortilla chips. Both carefully covered with a napkin and kept far away from Frankie.

It took me a while, but I finally decided I should give traditional meditation a go, as it has less bug appeal and is certainly less of a fire hazard. I chose a lazy Saturday afternoon and prepared first by reading a few chapters on meditation in a book by the Dalai Lama, and I felt inspired. He'd written that meditation is the way to a more meaningful life, and I could use some of that.

I closed the book and settled into a spot on the bed. My heart was racing! The very idea of meditation has always made me nervous, jumpy even. Just sit there and try not to think? Trying not to think is like me trying not to blink—it just makes me blink faster. With my back straight, I tried to get into a pretzel-legged pose, but I was hindered by my thighs (definitely don't want to think about that for too long), so I just sat kind of cross-legged on the bed and tried to breathe in and out in slow, serious meditation breaths. Five seconds in, my ear began to itch. I wondered if in the entire course of my life my ear had ever itched so intensely. I wondered what meditating people do about itching. Surely they have itchy moments? Do you scratch, and if so, do you have to start out all over again, or do those first four seconds count? The Dalai Lama had not addressed this. All that thinking about itching suddenly made my elbow itch, the left one. Who gets an itchy elbow? I wondered if I were meditating on itching. Finally I gave up, scratched, shook it off, and tried again. I had lasted nine seconds, give or take a few.

Settling back into my almost-cross-legged pose, I closed my eyes and took a deep breath, a deep cleansing breath. The windows were open to get some fresh air in the house, and it smelled a little like fresh-cut grass and spring and not smoggy at all. What is smog anyway? Smoke and fog? Smut and fog? Soot and pog? That's when I remembered I had to get my car smog checked before the end of the month. I started to calculate how much that might cost me if I needed repairs to pass the emissions test. I thought about the time I cried when I failed my first smog check right after my divorce. Back then it seemed like the end of the world, and now I feel like it's all just part of doing business—if it fails I'll get it fixed—and I started to congratulate myself on how much I have grown and matured as a person and, OH SHIT, I AM SUPPOSED TO BE MEDITATING. Then: I JUST CUSSED DURING MEDITATION. SHIT!

I shook my head, trying to release my mind's steel-trap grip on the mental to-do list. I inhaled, deeply, a cleansing breath— one that contained a cat hair. That is when the sneezing started, just a tickle at first and then a trifecta of sneezes, so I ran into the bathroom for a Kleenex. I had never been so happy to sneeze in my life. I didn't realize how much meditating could take out of a person! I'd been so tense trying not to move or itch or think that I was sweating a little.

While I was in the bathroom I did a little drive-by moisturiz-ing, making sure to get my elbow nice and lotioned up to prevent further itching. I applied lip gloss, redid my ponytail, looked in the mirror for stray eyebrow hairs . . . and then I realized I was procrastinating about meditating. *Not good.*

Why couldn't I just sit still and think nothing for ten whole seconds? Just ten seconds! Other people can meditate. They talk about it like it's as easy as breathing, and when people talk about meditating or write about it, you'd think this meditation stuff was the simplest, humblest way to achieve enlightenment and peace and harmony, and I want that! I do! I want some simple, serene, quiet place that I can go to inside myself and find my center and be all Zen and clean from the inside out. I would much rather prefer to be all sweetness and light, especially at work when someone makes me fantasize about using my X-Acto knife to re-create the shower scene from *Psycho* with them in the Janet Leigh role. It would be so much better to smile secretively, and just let them be crazy while I remained unaffected, a calm harbor in a raging sea of insanity. I want to find balance and change the world through my peaceful example instead of honking at the woman waiting for a written invitation to turn left, or flipping off people in traffic with a bird on the down low, holding my finger below the dashboard but still sending them the finger. I would rather meditate than go to the dentist. Really.

I went back to the bedroom, my most serene room, and sat on my bed, the softest, most comfortable item in my entire house. I sat comfortably, abandoning the faux lotus. I sighed. Then I breathed in deeply and exhaled slowly and closed my eyes.

Then I fell asleep.

Two hours later a car alarm sounded right outside my open window and I woke up with a little startle. And for just a moment, I was hopeful. Had I been meditating? I turned and caught sight of myself in the mirrored closet doors. I had little pillow lines all upside one half of my face. And I'd been dreaming about a boat ride, so I ascertained that perhaps my "meditating" had so exhausted me that it turned into a Saturday afternoon nap.

Defeated, I rolled off the bed and wandered into the kitchen. I opened the refrigerator door and stared inside. I stood there for a good while, contemplating some cold noodles. It was the first time all day I felt completely calm. I probably go to the fridge ten times a day and just contemplate it. I don't really think of anything; in fact, it's one of the few times my mind is clear and free, just looking, just waiting, just standing there all peaceful and hopeful. When you stand in front of the refrigerator with the door open, you aren't really expecting anything or anticipating anything. You aren't making something happen; it's the most passive thing you do in a kitchen. Just stand. Stare. Breathe. Look at the noodles.

That's when it dawned on me that maybe this is my form of meditating. Maybe I am from a long line of people who find their peaceful, centered place right in front of the refrigerator. Of course, that also may have something to do with my difficulty maneuvering the Lotus pose. But no one ever sits in front of the open fridge with their legs all twisted up anyway. Plain old slouching will do just fine for my meditation. Open door, slouch comfortably, breathe, stare into the fridge. Let the calmness wash over you.

Eat cold noodles. Repeat as often as needed. Meditation complete.

Passports, Pocketbooks, and Pants

This year, I am actually looking forward to Valentine's Day. In other years I haven't paid much attention to it. I personally prefer my holidays to come with government-mandated vacation days, but I don't really get upset over a day devoted to chocolate, especially if that chocolate will all be half price at Rite Aid come Friday morning.

Work can be a little treacherous, especially in an office where every single woman on the floor is walking around carrying gigantic bouquets of roses and exotic flowers with phallic things pointing out the middle. Each bouquet showier than the last, each a pollinated, exaggerated display of affection. But I am happy for them. I can't bring flowers home anyway; the cats set upon them like a festive buffet, and no matter where I try to hide them, by morning the vase is tumped over and water is everywhere, and the once-lovely flowers are stripped down to the stems.

But this year on February 14, I will be getting on an airplane and traveling across the ocean to go to Italy *by myself*. I can't believe I'm going to do it. I don't even go to the movies by myself. It's not that I'm afraid of being alone; it's just so much cozier to stay home and watch movies on my own TV set and drink wine.

I've never had the guts or gumption to travel by myself—especially not to somewhere far-off, like another continent. I was scared it might be lonely or scary or hard, but I needed a vacation, a real vacation. And now the new year had arrived and I was trying to improve myself, become a better person, find a life's purpose. Maybe I would find it somewhere else.

The scary parts were pretty intimidating—alone, so far from home!—but the more I thought about taking a vacation, the more excited I became about the sheer possibilities of it. Being able to stay wherever I preferred, eat whatever I had a craving for, linger in a museum as long as I wanted with no one else to consider but me. No one else's tastes and itinerary to accommodate; maybe it was selfish to even consider. But oh, it sounded decadent and pleasurable to me. Maybe selfishness is a woefully misunderstood concept. Maybe my secret life's skill is being selfish, and I should use it for good, not evil.

Online travel websites are the best invention. I am completely lured by their charms, addicted by their promises of cheap airfares and discounted hotel rooms. For days I spent my lunch breaks at work clicking and surfing, and one day I found it—a single perfect ticket at a price so low I was practically being paid to fly their airline! And I bought it without any planning, consultation, pro/con lists, anything at all but impulse and that same old desire to see something new, smell something new, taste something new. Someplace I had never gone before with no memories of my past to follow me, someplace with ridiculously cheap airfare . . . someplace with wine. And someplace where people do as the Romans do—because they are Romans. In Rome. Roaming around Rome.

I wasn't planning on going there. I didn't really pick Rome as my destination; it kind of picked me. Its cheapness was reason enough. After I bought the ticket and made my hotel reservation, which took something like a grand total of thirty-four seconds, I thought about what I had just done and gasped a little. But I was excited, and I was determined.

Then I started researching my trip, *after I bought the ticket.* If I could go back in time and change just one thing about my first vacation alone, I would skip all the guidebooks and online travel forums and just show up with my little suitcase and big expectations and see what happens. But I am an armchair traveler first, so I went to the bookstore the night I bought the ticket, loaded up on travel books about Rome, and spent almost as much as a hotel night's stay on Italian phrase books, maps, and a little audio CD of traveler's Italian essentials. When I got home, I pulled on my pajamas, poured a glass of wine, and spread all my books on the bed and started reading. Two hours later I was in shock, and by the end of the week I was afraid I had made a grave error in judgment.

I discovered much too late that every guidebook and travel forum has an entire chapter or area devoted just to the perils of Rome. Apparently you arrive, immediately get pickpocketed, ripped off, and scammed, and there's graffiti everywhere and people are rude and *you might perish*. In fact, if you do enough lunchtime or late-night Web surfing to get information about Rome, you may begin to think that you are flying to a traffic-congested, pickpocket paradise that is nothing more than an expensive tourist trap of rip-offs, crime, and congestion.

Here is a direct quote from a guidebook I bought right after I purchased my nonrefundable ticket: "Beware of thieving gangs of children . . . Rome is rife with con artists, thieves, and rip-offs, so conceal all your valuables or be prepared to lose them."

But they apparently have world-renowned gelato. Thank God for that.

Since my ticket was nonrefundable, in the few weeks leading up to my trip, I just stopped reading any guidebooks. It's amazing how denial works, but it does. Part of the excitement in vacationing is just getting ready for it. Before long I had a list two pages long of vacation to-dos.

Topping my list was finding my passport. After twenty minutes of digging around in drawers and secret hiding places, I located it in the silverware drawer and checked it to make sure it hadn't expired. There I am on the first page, my little square picture laminated forever, freezing me in official government documentation. I was about ten years younger and so much more hopeful (I assume) and I had bangs—big, thick bangs that accentuate the roundness of my face and make me look like a cherubic twelve-year-old.

My passport is filled with stamps from all the vacations I took with my ex-husband and the one single trip I took with my girlfriends the year after my divorce. As I reminisced over when I had bangs, I realized the passport in my hands was set to expire in three weeks, which would safely get me to Italy but not back home. And good vacations usually end with one returning to the place of origin, especially for a bona fide homebody such as myself.

Finding the expedited U.S. Passport Renewal Form online was a breeze, and luckily, Los Angeles has an office in Westwood dedicated to nothing but processing passports. After filling out the paperwork and making the appointment, the only remaining hurdle in the Brand-new Passport Excitement was the government regulation passport *photo*.

After living for the ten years with the wall of bangs picture, and considering the situation with my California driver's license picture, the new passport photo became an issue of great importance. When I tell people that my driver's license photo is the worst of the worst of the worst, they all laugh and say, "Yeah right! Mine is the worst! I look fat/short/bald/flattened in mine!"

And this is a perfectly normal response and exactly what I would say if I were a normal person with the normally bad government-issued ID picture. Then I show them my driver's license as proof, and they all say the very same thing, "Oh yeah. YOU WIN." Sometimes it is followed by sad, pitying looks and the small glimmer of relief that their driver's license photo, no matter how unflattering, is at least better than mine.

Imagine a beady-eyed orange woman with bright red lipstick held in a painful grimace as the camera shoots her from an angle that captures both her nostrils in full detail. That's me. The image on my driver's license looks like *Aileen [Wuornos] Portrait of a Serial Killer* in Oompa Loompa Techno-orange. It's a real treat to show store clerks or airline security people my driver's license. They try not to make "the face"—the face that says, "HOLY CRAP! THAT IS BUTT-UGLY!"—and yet I see it. I see their little smirks.

This driver's license photo is so bad that in preparation for dying (eventually), I once picked out a flattering picture of myself that showed a tan, happy, thinner me from six years ago and made copies of it and sent it to all my friends and family members and made them swear under oath to all that is good and holy to use that picture in any news stories or obituaries about me. This might strike some folks as morbid, but if you have seen my driver's license picture, you understand. The person in that driver's license photo is a color *that doesn't even occur in nature.*

So, to avoid this smirch in my passport photo shoot, I spent a few days doing serious beauty work. I got my hair cut and highlighted, I spent two days wearing those gloppy whitening trays so my teeth would be sparkly white and pure, and I used acne-prevention soap preventively just in case my skin got word that photo-taking was in the day planner.

I picked out three turtleneck sweaters off the sale rack at Macy's, one in deep red, one in jewel blue, and one in forest green. I never wear turtlenecks, and these were the first turtleneck sweaters I had purchased in more than a decade, since I got word from one of those cruelly truthful fashion makeover shows that women with anything over a B cup generally look like Mount Vesuvius in a turtleneck. However, passport pictures don't capture the impenetrable barrier of breast created by the unflattering expanse of the turtleneck. They only show you from the shoulders up. Which means the *neck*. And the only way to well and truly deal with my uncanny ability to develop twelve necks in a picture is to ensconce them all in a turtleneck.

My plan—my neurotic virtuso—was to go to three different passport-picture-taking places and wear a different sweater in each one. Then I would select from the best of these pictures and it would follow me like a happy new friend on all my future adventures. There's me: independent woman with great passport picture getting stamped by a hunky Russian immigration control guy! There's me in the future, flashing my hot passport picture at the dashing yet understated guy in military dress welcoming me to Chile and handing me his phone number. Anything good could happen with a clean slate, a plane ticket, and a fantastic passport picture.

I got all made up, got my hair done just right, and went to the FedEx Kinko's near my house where they take digital pictures so you get to approve the image before it's printed. The passport-picture area is in a corner near the special-orders desk. When it was my turn, the girl behind the desk grabbed a big, boxy camera and we walked over to the corner. I sat in the chair in front of the grayish-blue curtain and smiled just like I had practiced in the bathroom mirror—not a huge smile that would make my eyes disappear, but just enough to look like I am having fun on vacation. The girl holding the passport photo-taking digital camera snapped her gum and said, "You can't smile."

"Pardon?"

"No smiling. New rules."

I was sure I must have misheard her. I wanted to ask her, *Do you know what I look like when I am not smiling? When I am not deflecting the largesse of my cheek area by a toothy grin? I look like a grim-faced reaper of doom.* Surely she was mistaken or stoned. Or both.

"Why can't I smile?" Then, "Oh! Do I have something in my teeth?"

"No," she said. "It's something to do with terrorism. The smiling messes up the database or something."

"But isn't smiling proof that one is surely not a terrorist?" I asked.

"Listen, you can smile if you want, but they won't take it." She snapped her gum again for emphasis.

I just sat there, befuddled. No smiling? Because of the terrorists? We already have to wrap our three-ounce sample bottles of shampoo in Ziploc baggies to neutralize their threat to our airline security. For goodness sake—we have to remove our shoes and walk where people tread with their bare, stinky, germ-encrusted feet! Now they've taken away the passport-photo smile?

As I sat there in my stupor, she took the picture. Then she laughed. "Uh, we should probably take another one."

And she took another one, and I looked at it and it was awful. And yet another. In fact, I can never return to that particular store again because I made that poor girl take eleven pictures of me, all of which looked like some frightening, flash-bulb, crazed, deer-in-the-headlights marshmallow head. I walked out empty-handed—no passport picture, no self-worth, and with only the sounds of snickering employees to usher me out the door.

Undeterred, I continued my quest. Altogether I went to passport-photo locations in three zip codes wearing my different-colored turtlenecks before I got one picture that would not elicit fear and shrieks when I showed it to my friends. I might be embarrassed at the excess of vanity if it weren't for my orange driver's license picture staring at me each day from my wallet with those beady eyes and huge nostrils. If you look at my driver's license at just the right angle, I look like an orange horse with red lipstick. There's vanity, and then there is self-preservation.

With my glossy, fake eyelashes sitting above my marshmallow face and my turtleneck hiding the many chins, my passport photo looks almost human. The new passport itself was ready just two days after I turned in the application. It is stiff and clean, unmarked, ready to see the world and start getting stamped. And I am finally a color that occurs in nature. It is a very good start to my first solo trip.

Two days before my trip, I woke up in the middle of the night in a sweat. What if I got robbed the moment I stepped off the airplane? What if the airlines lost my luggage? Who would help me? What if I hated the hotel? What if there were bedbugs? What if my phrase book used a version of Italian incomprehensible in Rome? What if my passport was stolen? *What if I got lonely?*

It's the middle-of-the night fears that get me. And it's

impossible to go back to sleep once the middle-of-the-night fears start. Sometimes when I can't stop the chattering in my brain, I get out a pen and a piece of paper and I write it all down—every worry and every fear and every possible scenario of doom. Then after I record every free-floating anxiety (and it can take some time, you know; I've had five pages single-spaced, back and front of worry!), I write down exactly how I wish the event/trip/conversation would go. After I'm done, I fold the whole thing up and put it away in a shoe box. These are my letters to the Universe.

One day, after I'm long gone, someone's going to find that shoebox and have a hearty laugh at Ye Olde Crazypants. But it helps me in the moment to get all the worry out of my head and into someone else's capable hands—in this case, the shoe box's. So I wrote it all down, every crazy fear, every dumb worry, every whiny, crybaby, worst-case scenario. Then I wrote, "I just want to have a relaxing Valentine's Day in Rome with no bedbugs or robberies. The end."

On Turning into My Mother, Your Mother, and Her Mother, Too

Flying is not my favorite thing to do. I get anxious. My hands tremble. My heart beats so loud it's audible over the roar of the airplane engines. Sometimes I freak out and grab the hand of whoever is sitting next to me, which must reassure them and make them feel needed.

A few days before my trip, I went to visit my doctor for some chemical help with my airplane-flying problems. I needed to see Dr. Curt, because I believe in better living through chemistry, and also, I needed him to check out my left arm because I might have a tumor.

I am always and forever showing up to the doctor's office with interesting ailments. Such as the time I had dry skin and thought it was scabies. Or the time I was sure I had a melanoma and it turned out to be a pimple. I am often told to stop looking up weird shit on WebMD, but I can't help it. The Internet is just so useful for diagnosing things!

"Hey, Dr. Curt, can you also look at my arm tumor?"

"You have an arm tumor?" he asked. "You just spent twenty minutes talking about germs on airplanes, but an arm tumor is just a 'Hey, by the way' issue? Okay, let me see the alleged tumor," he said. I pulled up my left shirtsleeve so he could see the odd, lumpy upper arm.

"Is it fatal?" I asked.

"It's not fatal," he sighed. "It's called a muscle."

"But I don't have any muscles," I assured him. "There must be some mistake."

"You aren't dying," he told me. "*Once again.* It's just your arm muscle."

"But why would I have a muscle only on one arm?" I asked. "The other arm is just as flabby and disgusting as ever."

"Well," he said. "Are you left-handed?"

"Nope."

"Do you carry anything heavy on that arm?"

"Nope."

He looked around the small white examination room, and his eyes came to rest on the chair in the corner, where my giant black handbag was oozing.

"How much does your purse weigh?" he asked. And before I could intervene, or lie, or even roll down my left shirtsleeve, the good doctor was measuring my handbag, setting it on the scale and weighing the beast. I am not one to be sizest or to advocate dieting at all, but my handbag needs Weight Watchers ASAP.

"It weighs 14.2 pounds," Dr. Curt said.

"That is just sad," I replied, and then sighed. "I have officially turned into my mother."

"Well, now we know where your mysterious bodybuilding is coming from," he said. I do believe he chuckled.

It hasn't always been this way. When I was younger, I used my pockets for my lipstick and change. Later, in college, I had one of those ID sleeves where you keep money too, and then I still put my lipstick in my pocket. You know why? My face was perkier back then. Back then my five-year plan included "Go on spring break in a bikini!" I did not need the concealer, pressed powder, mascara, and lip-plumping gloss of today.

After college, when I started working at real jobs, I got a real pocketbook filled with lipstick, compact, car keys, wallet, and gum. When I moved to Los Angeles, it stayed the same—until my germ issues intensified. My handbags carried all the above plus Handi Wipes and Kleenex. No woman should be without Kleenex.

Then cell phones came along, and you had a cellular telephone the size of a shoe inside your pocketbook, plus a charger and car charger, and this was fine, because *Look at me! I am so cool! I have a shoe phone!* I remember calling my friend Stefanie back home in Tennessee and saying, "Stef! I am talking to you from my car! Can you believe it! Can you hear me?"

Then somewhere in my mid-to-late twenties I graduated to real purses. I got a husband, and funny how it worked out that I was always carrying his stuff around, too. Sunglasses, wallet, cell phone—luggage for two!

Then I got divorced and was wearing my sweatpants backward and do not remember how I got to the liquor store and back, but I can only assume I carried my money in a Ziploc baggie. (True, sadly.) Then I had a moment of "I should buy that expensive, beautiful handbag I cannot afford because I am spurned, and it will accompany me everywhere." I bought it, and it was a very lovely handbag. I bought a wallet for it, and a sunglasses case and an emery board.

Now, after all this time, I carry a monster. My mother saw it one day and laughed at me because my new handbag eclipsed hers, and she is a hunchback from years of hauling around handbags the size of beach totes. *Hi, Mom! I have turned into you! And I have your handbag.* Along with forty-nine emery boards, two travel-size packages of Kleenex, eleventy-seven pieces of paper, a notebook, eighty-two business cards, four packs of gum, and probably the final resting place of Jimmy Hoffa.

I secretly get a huge feeling of smug pleasure every time someone asks me, "Do you have a so-and-so . . . ?" and I dig around in my handbag of hugeness and sure enough, I HAVE IT IN MY BAG! I always feel just like I have produced cold fusion or something anytime that happens. And now I am growing muscles, too, in my left arm. I feel so proud.

Traveling by the Seat of My Fat Pants

Sixteen hours before I got on the plane and flew to Rome, I panicked. Not about pickpockets, or bag-snatchers, or the dismal currency rate, or the airplane crashing into fiery pieces above Greenland—I panicked about my pants.

The Great Pants Disaster happened in my bedroom in Encino, California, the night before my Big Solo Escape from Valentine's Day Adventure. My suitcase was open on the bed and I had neat piles of clothes separated on the bedspread like satellite countries, an outfit for every single day of my upcoming vacation. Shirts, socks, and underwear were all lined up in their respective piles: Thursday, Friday, Saturday, and Sunday clothes, plus an outfit for the trip home and a spare. Nothing brings out the "belle genome" from careful hiding like the experience of packing for a trip. My accent gets thicker, my attention to accessorizing heightens, and every item is divided into neat packing cubes or individual Ziploc baggies. Shoes and outfits must be coordinated and there *will be room* for both the curling iron and the necessary power adaptor and transformer. The only thing missing in all this organizing and carrying-on were my pants.

Somehow, in the four weeks or so prior to my big adventure, I had managed to beef up and add a fine layer of protective fat all around my body. I had grown at least one if not two pants sizes, moving away from my "I bought these in the normal misses' department" jeans into my Lane Giant pants.

You do not need a couch and a framed Ph.D. in psychology to see that the search for life purpose that I had rigorously put myself on at the beginning of the year had stirred up something inside me, prompting me to pre-eat for the journey and thus gain some weight. None of the pants I wore just a month ago fit me now without causing the blood to stop circulating to my extremities. Maybe I was tapping into an instinctual survival mechanism: store fat prior to long journeys.

I had no idea why I'd gained weight like that, putting on twelve pounds in six weeks' time. For the few months prior to Christmas, I had managed to stay on a pretty even keel. I wasn't back down to my pre-divorce skinny jeans yet, but I also hadn't been wearing the size 18 and 20 plain black pants of grief. I had been able to buy jeans in a regular department store, too, and not in the women's department (a size 14, but that's average. I was thrilled.). The weight I'd gained from stopping smoking was explainable, but this padding was new. What had happened to me? What was going on in there?

The answer wasn't clear, but the problem was. One simply cannot walk around Europe on her very first Big Solo Adventure without any pants on. It was February, for one thing. And it was probably illegal, for another. I had to dig out the fat pants from the back of the closet and carefully pack four identical pairs of Lane Bryant size 16 black trousers into my suitcase. Plus one extra, in charcoal gray.

I packed the suitcase, fat pants included, left out a detailed and ridiculously long note for my cat sitter ("Bob has a new hiding place in the bedroom closet, so please leave the closet door halfway open at all times!!"), and the next morning I boarded a plane bound for Italy.

The time in the air was uneventful, and the little helper my doctor prescribed me kept me from mauling the woman in the seat beside me during takeoffs and landings. I watched the in-flight movie, knitted a little on a hat I'd brought with me, and slept a few hours.

We arrived just on time. I made sure the guy behind the glass in the passport-control line stamped my passport, and I collected my luggage and found my way to the hotel. Much to my delight and surprise, the guidebooks were wrong—nary a thieving gang of children greeted me at the airport. What greeted me instead were the most beautiful people I have ever seen on earth.

Everyone in Italy is *gorgeous*. The guys emptying the trash at the airport were hot. The women sweeping the streets were beautiful—and in stilettos. I don't like to generalize about an entire population, but clearly I had landed in the middle of a Versace ad. The motor cops wear designer uniforms, for Pete's sake!

As it turned out, I loved Rome. The scariest part was all my pre-worrying ahead of time, especially since I couldn't tell anyone I was scared, since I was being brave and was saving face. But once I was there I felt completely fine, much safer than most places in Los Angeles. Just like anywhere, I didn't plant my big-ass black patent leather purse out on the table and walk away, but I didn't see one thieving gang. It was loud and busy, and it was also vibrant and exciting and unbelievably beautiful. I guess I have lived in Los Angeles and worked downtown for so long that traffic, grime, graffiti, and panhandlers just round out the scenery. There's this crazy juxtaposition of ancient things (a structure built in AD 27) with brand-new Ducati motorbikes parked out front, or plazas with amazing Bernini-sculpted fountains surrounded by girls in leather jackets and spike-heel knee boots. There's the Pantheon—and McDonald's directly outside it.

Cities and towns and even whole countries have a vibe to them, and whenever I land somewhere new, I always try to tune in to it, feel it out. I can definitely see why some folks prefer one destination over another—there are people who really only feel centered near the water, or near mountains, or those who prefer New York to anywhere else, or Key West—and isn't that the point of traveling anyway? You see new things and develop new preferences and learn about the world and yourself. Don't you travel to see, learn, smell, taste, taste again, taste some more, and expand your life? Rome was definitely an expansion for me. The city was pulsing like a heart, loud like Los Angeles, older than anything I have ever seen or imagined, holy, tacky, beautiful, tasty—and everyone there is gorgeous.

Traveling alone wasn't nearly the scary, lonely experience I'd feared it might be. At the hotel I carefully inspected the bed for bedbugs, and, reassured that I was alone in the room, I hung up my clothes and took a long, hot shower. I went out that first afternoon in Rome and walked and walked until I found a restaurant calling my name. I ate a hearty bowl of pasta and drank a glass of wine and then walked some more. The city is compact and crowded, with more motorbikes than cars. And everywhere you look people are talking on their cell phones, or pushing baby strollers, or walking purposefully to somewhere, all in the shadows of ancient buildings, fountains, and ruins.

Initially, I was painfully shy about asking people to take my picture at the big touristy landmarks, but after the first few times, it ended up being a highlight. I'd try to pick people who were also tourists, usually couples, and I'd ask the woman half of the couple to take my picture, and then afterward I'd offer to use their camera to get a picture of them for their own memories (that was something I learned from all those years of vacationing as part of a couple; you get very few pictures of the two of you together on vacation), and everyone was happy with this traveler's exchange. In some incredibly dorky way, I felt like I was part of someone else's good vacation memories, too. And it was easier, especially if I heard a tourist couple speaking Spanish, French, or English, so I knew I could communicate. My Italian turns out to be limited to "Wine, please," which worked surprisingly well for me in restaurants but is not so descriptive in picture-taking.

Almost every Italian person I met in Rome spoke fluent English, more so than just about any city I have visited. I did know how to order a few things in Italian and how to say "please" and "thank you," but for the most part, shop owners, waiters, and clerks speak to everyone who does not immediately appear to be an Italian in clear, lilting English.

The trip could have lasted twice as long and I would have loved it. Traveling alone was scary, awesome, exhilarating, exhausting, relaxing, and most of all made me feel like I could conquer the world. I didn't think I could really do it—travel all by myself to a strange place and navigate it solo—but I did. It had its lonely moments and its surprising moments, and most of all, it was just my tiny, little adventure that I always secretly wanted to do.

The very best things about traveling alone are that you get to move fully at your own pace and it's easy to meet people if you get lonely. You're on no one's timetable but your own, maybe for the first time ever! I spent one entire day in Rome just people-watching, walking around, and having good meals. I did not take a tour, learn anything useful, or apply myself to history and context on that day. It was probably one of my favorite days in my entire life.

Knitting the Light Fantastic

Every few weeks I come down with a case of craft flu. When Drew and I made our vision boards, I realized I had reached the very zenith of my existence, combining my love of self-help busywork with my deep need to glue and cut and create something I will later hide in a closet.

When I was a child my parents could take me anywhere, as long as they brought along a book or something I could fold, color on, or cut into snowflakes. We used to spend every summer at a lake in Texas called Possum Kingdom, and all summer long I would dig around in the clay along the shore and make gloppy sculptures that baked out in the Texas sun until a rainstorm dissolved each one back into the mud.

When my dad took us out in the boat and wanted to keep me quiet, he'd hand me some faded driftwood and his pocketknife, and I would whittle. I was seven. Remarkably, I still have all my fingers. Back then there were no twenty-four-hour-a-day cable networks devoted to showing real-life emergency room traumas, so children in the 1970s did things like whittle with pocket-knives and swim in murky creeks while all the adults got drunk and listened to country music.

My brother used to bring me home from a neighbor's house each day on the handlebars of his bicycle, and this was normal and expected. Now, of course, bicycle helmets and safety seats are mandatory, and kids are belted and strapped in and padded at all times. Today childhood seems fragile and tinged with peril, but mine was sturdy and largely unsupervised, and we all survived and flourished. On our long car rides to Possum Kingdom, my brother and I would stand up on the backseat and wave at passing truckers. Then we'd hit each other for two hours until one of us got tired or started bleeding.

The night before the trip I would pack up all my dolls, stuffed animals, books, and doodads, we'd load up the car, and the next morning we'd drive to Possum Kingdom and stay in a rented camper for a few weeks. It was the best part of the whole summer. There was an old guy, Elmer, who lived on a barge at the lake, and he loved all things Budweiser. He drank a fine amount of the king of beers, decorated his houseboat with Budweiser stuff, and wore pants with Budweiser cans printed on them—I adored him.

He treated all the kids like miniature adults and cursed in front of us, and he had a shaggy dog he would let me play with all summer as if it were my own dog. Elmer had a hat with Budweiser cans sewn into it, and he wore it every day like a crown. He would let me draw Budweiser cans on all his place mats and once let me make him a collage of Parliament cigarette boxes from all the empties he cleaned from the car.

My childhood was filled with long hours spent gluing weird stuff onto construction paper. During elementary school I started sewing. I joined 4-H and tried to win the bandana bikini sewing competition. I didn't win, but I got an honorable mention, and that was enough to keep me sewing for years, dressing all my dolls in handmade gauchos and shirts cut from the remnants of my dad's old ties.

I've decoupaged, painted, stenciled, and scrapbooked. I've made dollhouses and assembled model cars and airplanes, and once, at Vacation Bible School, I made a sculpture entirely out of macaroni. When pottery painting shops were the newest fad, my house was filled with my collection of hand-painted ceramic tissue holders, jewelry boxes, and vases. I've mosaiced, glue-gunned, and papier-mâchéd.

Yarn-related crafts entered my life at a relatively late age. My paternal grandmother was an avid crocheter and her house was filled with crocheted doilies and generic Barbie-type dolls wearing crocheted hoopskirts to cover a roll of toilet paper. There were crocheted Christmas ornaments, a crotched toilet paper cover, and one year she created a multicolored crocheted poodle to cover the vacuum cleaner when it wasn't in use. Until my friends started knitting and got me to a knitting class, I still assumed all yarn came in candy-corn-colored skeins that caused your skin to itch when you got too close to them.

Once I got past my fear of turning into a doily factory like my grandma, knitting cannibalized all my other crafts. There is an entire wall in my home office dedicated to yarn, color-coded and divided by brand and fiber, all stored carefully in plastic snap-lid tubs. There is chunky yarn for quick projects, pure wool for felting, and colorful acrylic that has been engineered over the years to feel as soft as angora.

My knitting projects are almost uniformly boring, mostly scarves that I get to wear for ten minutes each January. But I love the *activity* of knitting. It starts with picking out a yarn and finding some needles that work well with it or experimenting. Knitting swatch after swatch in different needle sizes is a fine pastime. I try to use patterns, but that requires concentration and effort, so I often end up knitting mindlessly in front of the TV or on the bus, acres of smooth, pleasing stockinette or bumpy garter stitch that I bind off and admire smugly and then stick in a drawer.

Knitting is not just an activity, though; it's an entire community. People knit together and gather weekly into groups who sit around a table with total strangers, comparing projects, yarns, or techniques. Before long, you find out you have more in common with someone than just a love of scarves, and before you know it, you're out shopping together or eating lunch, and one day you realize that most of your friends are other knitters. Maybe that's why knitting and crocheting have reemerged in our collective consciousness and haven't died the slow death of decoupage and sand paintings. When you spend fifteen hours a week commuting and all your days working in front of a computer monitor, the biggest social circle most of us have is online. Meeting other humans in real life through a shared activity is a natural urge.

Add wine and the creative high of crafting, and you've got a social phenomenon.

Like all cults, knitting and crocheting have their different flavor of followers. There are your dabblers, your experts, and your competitive stitchers. And then there are sock knitters. People who knit socks live in a world with tiny needles and complicated heel turns and grafted seams, and they are interesting to me in the way high-level mathematicians are. They fascinate and intimidate me. While I can't even calculate sales tax, I admire those who walk around with theorems in their heads and equations that explain it all. I just don't want them to ask me any questions, or I might start babbling nervously about how cool it is that glue comes in a stick. This is how I initially felt about sock knitters.

I had never given much thought to the functional, omnipresent sock until I started knitting. My wardrobe requires socks on a regular basis, but I really didn't think about how they were constructed, or even how they fit. I have low-cut, plain white tennis socks, one or two pairs of cutesy socks—Halloween comes to mind—and a drawerful of basic athletic socks. I might own a trouser sock or two, and if I am not mistaken, one lonely pair of argyle kneesocks sits in the corner of my sock drawer, waiting anxiously for the 1980s to make a roaring comeback. In the '80s I had a tragic and short-lived romance with neon socks. I would layer my colorful socks over each other, and then over my jeans. With the shoulder pads in all my tops and the painstakingly pegged jeans, I looked like an inverted triangle with bright, multicolored feet.

Aside from a blip in the '80s neon era, the lowly sock has been nothing more than a stretchy fabric cover-up for my bad pedicure days. And even when I first started knitting, I passed right over the sock yarns because I don't really *need* cozy hand-knit socks here in the arctic wilds of Southern California. This is almost exclusively flip-flop country. Then again, I don't really need my hand-knit scarves and hats and mittens (mittens! Really now!), and not even the scorching summer heat has stopped me from knitting like garter stitch was about to be banned by the government. I guess I just hadn't considered that people with access to inexpensive, mass-produced Walmart socks actually choose to knit them instead, not until I took up knitting myself and met Them: the Sock People.

Eventually they found me and talked soothingly to me, and told me stories about how easy it was and how quick, portable, and fulfilling sock knitting could be. I'm sluttish and easy when it comes to craft cults, so it didn't take much convincing. After all, I assured myself, it's just yarn. If I messed up somewhere in the middle and made a heel of myself—heel!—no one was going to show up on my doorstep and take me into custody for crimes against knitting. Probably.

So I fell into the snare of these sock-knitting enthusiasts. I bought a pattern and some yarn and some emergency wine, just in case. I started with a swatch, which is a very good place to start, especially when one is an insanely cramped, tight knitter. From the scrunched-up little stitches on my needles, most people safely assume I took up knitting as a mode of therapy, which is not far from the truth. I am working out some issues on that yarn. Swatches have become a part of my life, knitting little squares and measuring them with small craft rulers manufactured expressly for the purpose of measuring stitches. When I finally found the correct needle size for the pattern's required gauge (two needle sizes bigger than the pattern called for), I cast on and started my first sock cuff.

Casting on was relatively painless, a simple knit-one-purl-one ribbing. *So easy! I can do this!* Socks are small, round projects, and anything like that requires a special kind of needle with points on both ends (double-pointed needles or DPNs, as they're known in the world of knitting). Working with double-pointed needles kind of makes you feel like you're doing Xtreme Knitting and you should be televised for ESPN.

The honeymoon phase—the cuff and body of the sock—lasted about two bus rides. When I got to the part of the pattern where it dawned on me that I was not making a tube sock and needed to turn the heel, I was bumping along in rocky traffic with my pattern slipping off my lap, my stitch counter rolling around on the seat, and some strong language forming in my mind. After about fifteen minutes of slipped stitches and almost poking my seatmate in the eye, it dawned on me that I was doing this intentionally, making a heel flap on a moving, lurching metro bus, and yet as far as I recollect, I have never suffered a head injury, or been tortured, or spent an extended period in a coma.

The stressful knitting incident on the bus taught me an important lesson: sit somewhere quiet, placid, and full of stable, nonmoving surfaces when you turn a heel. Good information to know! There should be a plaque somewhere or a needlepoint sampler with that bit of wisdom on it.

My first heel turned, quietly at home, and I began to notice that this whole sock-knitting endeavor is a little bit like making pure magic. Here you have some sticks and some string and all of a sudden, you have—oh my word—IT IS A HEEL! It is very exciting. I tried to share my excitement with my coworkers.

"Hey, I know we're in a meeting to discuss a spreadsheet, but you guys! Guess what? I made a sock!"

"Hi Joe. Yes I got the ad request you filled out—hey, have you seen my hand-knitted sock?"

I felt as if I had single-handedly built Stonehenge or something. Picking up stitches, knitting halfway through a row and back again, shaping the heel with short rows, and yet all of it just using basic knit and purl stitches with a few increases and decreases. It was astonishing. I wondered if I were maybe a knitting prodigy.

"Really! I know we're supposed to be corporate and on-task and having a meeting about the department's budget for the coming year, but look at my SOCK!"

I made it through the heel flap, through a cat chewing one of my double-pointed needles, through three rows mistakenly knit on the wrong side, and through my first gusset. By the time I reached the toe, I was so full of myself that my knitting ego had to ride shotgun in the car.

"I MADE A WHOLE SOCK!" I informed my dad. "A whole, entire sock! By hand! With just yarn and knitting needles!"

"That's great," my dad said. "But don't you have two feet?"

Ah. Here's the one thing the Sock People forget to mention when they convert you to their religion. You'll love knitting up a sock; you'll love how portable and fast and addictive they can be. You'll be amazed at your own skills and dexterity for picking up stitches where none have ever existed. What they don't tell you is that the second sock is a lonely, desolate outpost of obligation. That second sock is just the stepchild of the first sock's exuberance. Oh, the second sock! It takes forever and a day to finish it. By the time I cast off the last stitch and weaved in all my little yarn ends, I had lost the first sock. It turned up weeks later at the bottom of my laptop bag.

Once I had the pair, I would show them to people, brag about my socks, tell my friends how easy it was, how surprised I was to see it all come together, shaped exactly like a regular old sock! But from my knitting needles! I felt the excitement my grandmother must have experienced when she covered all her toilet paper rolls in little crocheted skirts. It was the euphoric high of a completed craft project.

What I didn't tell people is that I was too afraid of messing up my hand-knit socks to actually wear them. They're too pretty. And to this day they sit in my sock drawer, folded neatly in a pile of variegated pink and purple wool-blend yarn. They are still lovely and perfect and unworn, and they are all mine.

Resolution #4:
Go on a Real Live Date

Summer Lovin' Had Me a Blast

My birthday sits almost exactly halfway through the calendar year. I think this is good timing, and every year I do some navel-gazing and list-making and see where I am in my yearly quest toward self-improvement. Sometimes I make a list of things I have accomplished to make me feel less old and afraid of smartphones. Sometimes the list reveals areas where I could use some gentle nudging. This is how I discovered on the morning of my birthday that I had not been on a date since the earth was still a molten ball.

I've been busy, I tell myself. *I'm not looking for a long-term commitment,* I tell my friends. But the truth is I am lazy, and dating is work. I haven't ever been a divorced woman of my age before, so I'm not sure what exactly I am supposed to be doing, but I deeply suspect I am failing in the relationship department. Six months have passed since my last date, and in your thirties, I think that's dog years multiplied by five.

That's how my Relationship Resolution started. It was my birthday, and my friend Faith took me out for dinner and drinks and then more drinks, and while we were waiting for the valet, a guy in line was kind of hitting on me. I didn't realize it until several hours later when I was home alone painting my toenails while one of my cats chased a hair barrette. And just like that I thought, *Hey, that guy was hitting on me.*

And I sighed because I felt like I was just not living up to my singleness potential. *Okay, fine. I'll give it a try. Just for the summer.* It's like learning to drive or ride a bike—you never forget. You fall off, you get back up, and so on.

On the Prowl with Jimmy Carter

There are some good things to be said about reentering the world of dating as your midthirties self, who is both free from teenage immaturity and also worldly enough to have been engaged and married but also divorced and thoroughly familiar with stipulated judgments and divorce court bailiffs. The one high point of such maturity and experience is that you are no longer looking for Mr. Perfectly Right, since all your Cinderella fantasies played out more like the scary winter scenes from *The Shining,* with no ax-murdering but just as crazy.

So, with your new perspective on men and relationships in general, you may find yourself at a new place, a place where you fool yourself into thinking you're just doing a statistical sampling of the dating population before you really dive in, but in fact you're just dating completely inappropriate men because you don't have to marry them. They skipped that chapter in the promise-ring pamphlet! Because no longer are you implanted with the teenage and early-adulthood homing device set to "Find Husband." Or perhaps it's there, but now the dial is pointing to "Have Fun While Boobs Are Still Round."

Your internal clock that used to tick out an image of you as Cinderella at the wedding altar has already ticked and tocked and then died a slow death. Your untethered, single clock, however, is right on time.

But even fun, frivolous things have a drawback. Like pie. Pie is delicious, enticing, tempting, and definitely available for a fling. But have you ever tried to eat an entire pie? I have, with disastrous results. One cannot expect every fun and tasty thing to be good for them. But it is always good to take a scientific approach and use knowledge gained from trial and error (and perhaps more error) to form a final hypothesis. That was how I discovered that through the cruel forces of time I keep aging every year. Yet through the magic of evolution and antioxidants, I can be my age, and the age of my dating applicants can remain stationary. This sounds like heaven, but it can have some minor drawbacks. There are a few qualifying questions you may want to ask during your scientific exploration of the much-younger opposite sex.

One might think of qualifying questions as the things you ask to discover incompatibilities, such as red flags (sixteen children!) and prison records. And all of that should fill your basic chatty questionnaire, of course, followed by a deep background check if things go to a third date. Thanks be to the Internet and the power of the instant background check—the best dating tool money can buy.

But the qualifying details I am referring to are very simply meant to weed out the cute young men who might make me feel old and wrinkled and possibly grandmotherly before my time. *Maternal* is not a great feeling you want to have on a first date.

The first time I discovered the need for filtering mechanisms for my potential dates started out innocently enough. I was at a Mexican restaurant with the cute guy from the produce department at Whole Foods Market. He'd helped me find the organic strawberries and later I gave him my phone number. So far what I knew about him could fill a postcard: vegetarian, student, played guitar. Soft brown eyes. Nice hands. Likes animals.

We were eating our dinner and talking about the week ahead, and I mentioned I was disappointed I had to miss a Habitat for Humanity event that my company sponsored.

"I had a presentation at work that day," I told my date, "so I was really sad that I couldn't go. Jimmy Carter was there with his wife Rosalynn and the team got to meet them. Plus, I've never done a Habitat for Humanity thing, which would have been exciting in itself, you know, to see if I could manage to wield a hammer without accidentally murdering a fellow volunteer."

"Well, maybe next time," said my date. Who was twenty-four. With the soft brown eyes.

"I know . . . it's just that you don't get a chance to meet a former U.S. president very often," I said into my salad.

"Which president?" he asked.

"Uh, Jimmy Carter . . ." I said.

"That dude wasn't president," said my date. Out loud.

"Of which country?" I asked. "Because he was president of the United States. Remember . . . peanut farmer from Georgia? First U.S. president to win the Nobel Prize after leaving the presidency? Billy Beer?"

Blank stare.

Then, *Oh God, of course he doesn't remember; he was born after the invention of cell phones that didn't require a Sherpa.*

Then, *Oh God, I am really old.*

Then, *Oh, Divine Power, help me find a way out of this date expediently and with the least amount of kissing possible. I cannot be on a date with someone who was born during a year I can remember living through. I cannot swap spit with a kid who doesn't know that Jimmy Carter was president. Amen.*

My date ended, finally, awkwardly. I am either extremely superficial or not superficial enough, because my date's cuteness faded away over dinner right after I explained there were actually two George Bushes. And the worst part of the entire date was that while I did manage to miss the good-night kiss, I would have to either switch grocery stores or shop only on Thursdays between 8:00 AM and noon.

After some time to reflect, though (and to find a new grocery store), I have decided I am grateful to have had that experience, because now I am sure to work in a casual, "Can you name the last seven U.S. presidents?" into the basic predate flirtation. You would be surprised how handy that information can be.

Dating in the Wireless Wilderness

The first horseman of the apocalypse is undoubtedly the Internet personal ad.

I am not sure why every single personal ad on the Internet is some variation of: "Balding, paunchy, twice-divorced, unemployed male seeks independently wealthy supermodel, thin with large breasts, for no strings attached fun. Nonsmokers only."

I'm exaggerating, but only a little. Some guys dress it up better than others, as in: "Eclectic creative guy seeks athletic, free-spirited equal; let's see what happens." Or: "Nice guy wants to explore his naughty side with slim, attractive woman over eighteen."

Like many people, I once thought online dating might hold some promise. Online dating has been around long enough now so that it's not quite the smarmy, seedy, technopervy way of meeting people that it used to be. Just a few years ago it was embarrassing and slightly pathetic to admit you'd met someone through the computer. Now it's almost a badge of honor: "Look! I survived online dating and met someone who isn't a sex addict! We do have to play World of Warcraft for six hours every weekend, but that is a small price to pay for true love!"

And believe me, I have heard the great stories about online dating and how well it worked for so-and-so; for example, how Neal in the software division met his wife online and now they have a three-bedroom house in Orange County and a daughter named Emma or Lily. And how Melissa in accounting met a guy online and now they're about to go on a trip to New Zealand to take the Hobbit tour. I'm an optimist at heart, and I decided that I would think positively and maybe I would meet some nice guy who didn't try to tie me up; and if all else failed, I would have some funny stories to tell my married friends when they had fights with their husbands.

Just in case you were wondering, all else failed.

I thought joining an online dating service would be sort of like a dating catalog, kind of like online shopping, where you browse the merchandise and look for what might be a good fit, and then you send them a note and so on, and you could do all this browsing from home without ever having to step foot into a bar or a club where half the women are wearing dresses the size of cocktail napkins.

As it turns out, online dating is a lot like dating in 3-D. Men prefer to be the ones browsing the catalog and making the first move. And online they can do it en masse. Each man can send a heartfelt personal note to sixty-five women at one time. It is a marvel of modern technology. And coincidentally, online people lie just as well as—if not better than—they do in real life. "Separated" often means "We live in the same house and my wife and I are separated by the wall as she makes dinner in our kitchen."

Many of the services have basic bullet points you can answer to let others know your marital status, employment status, how many kids you have, and so on. If the response to any of the standard bullets is "I'll Tell You Later," this means the answer is something you don't want to hear. And creative "aw-shucks" first-timer lingo, such as "just trying this out to see how it goes" often means "I am exploring my options online while my wife thinks I am job hunting."

In the world of online dating, the goods are not as well-described as in the world of online shopping. For example, any man who says he is five foot seven is actually five foot four. I know this because I am five foot almost four, and each of the five foot seven men I met were remarkably right at my eye level when I was wearing flats. For a while I assumed this meant I had grown taller to go with my curvy physique, but after a few coffee dates, I realized I was still short—and so were they.

I don't mind a short guy. Or a bald guy. Especially if they can name the last seven U.S. presidents. But it took me a while to get the lingo of online dating. Just like "curvy" is code for "a little fat" on a woman's profile, five foot seven is code for "five foot five and under" on a male profile. And people always post the most flattering picture ever taken of them, usually from a few years ago, when they were just out of puberty and still had the robust glow of youth. I wish I would have known that last detail; I would have found my emergency obituary photo and posted that instead of a current unretouched picture of myself. For some reason I had the misguided notion we were supposed to be honest about appearances to save any unnecessary awkwardness at the first meeting. How naive of me!

Online dating is just as murky and full of lemons as finding a used car in the classifieds. Once you learn the lingo, it's easier to spot the models with high mileage and no warranty. Guys looking for "a good time" just want to get lucky. Ditto "no strings attached," "looking for fun," and "let's keep it simple." These are all code words for "I want to have sex with anonymous Internet women who will split the check at dinner." Guys who are "artistic" and "creative" are working sporadically while waiting for their big break in Hollywood. They prefer women with a steady income, naturally. Guys who wink, or nudge, or whatever cutesy term the service uses for "I saw your profile and am too lazy to e-mail you" are also too lazy to call you.

Perhaps online dating works well for some people because they have the perfect combination of stamina and luck and are able to find that one used car—I mean, personal ad—that exposes the diamond in the rough. I don't have great dating stamina. I found mostly lemons.

But I am to blame for this, of course. For one thing, I posted an accurate picture of myself. The first guy I met in person told me, "Oh, you look just like your picture." His tone was sad, deflated. He'd truly expected me to improve in the flesh. We managed to complete fifteen minutes of small talk in a North Hollywood diner before we both remembered we each had pressing appointments to get to on a Sunday at 1:30 in the afternoon.

The biggest problem I had with online dating was that my ability to write witty and charming e-mails far exceeded my ability to create witty and charming chitchat in person. People who enjoy writing should stick to writing the personal ads of their friends and leave online dating to those who can endure blind-date chitchat over and over and over again.

ONLINE DATING: A TALLY

DATE 1: Guy who was disappointed that I looked like my picture

DATE 2: Guy who said he was divorced but was still married

DATE 3: Guy who asked me if I wanted to meet at his place. When I said I wanted to meet for coffee, he canceled date. Not really a date.

DATE 4: Tried to interest me in a pyramid scheme

DATE 5: Guy who talked for twenty minutes about how many people had "friended" him on Facebook. When I said I wasn't on Facebook, he made fun of me and pointed out that even his grandmother was on Facebook. Then he suddenly remembered he was supposed to be somewhere.

(SWITCHED ONLINE DATING SERVICES)

DATE 6: The one who wanted me to run lines with him for his upcoming audition. Then he complained that I wasn't putting enough emotion into the role of "Tom."

DATE 7: Guy who talked about his ex-wife the whole date

DATE 8: Guy who wanted to know if I'd ever been in a threesome or would consider it

(CLOSED ONLINE DATING ACCOUNT)

More Pitfalls of the Plugged-In

Andy is forty-three, and that alone makes him a more appropriate date than I've had in months. He's employed, and not at my local grocery store, so I don't have to worry about changing stores yet again. We met at a flea market; he was there looking for oldies and treasures for his online auction side business, which I thought was a great hobby. It sure beats other traditional Los Angeles hobbies like attending porn conventions or stealing car radios. I thought Andy was a really nice guy. He was sane, had funny stories, and seemed genuinely nonfreaky. He was nice. Then he googled me and everything changed.

On our third date Andy suddenly started calling me "baby" and acting like the Marlboro Man. The nice Jewish boy I'd met at the flea market had morphed into a hands-on, tough-talking, film noir character with octopus arms. I had no idea what was happening. It was like watching a very intense high-school drama production—you have no idea why you keep watching or what's happening, *but you cannot turn away.*

We were at dinner that night, at Jerry's Deli in Tarzana. Jerry's Deli is a Los Angeles landmark, a bright, chaotic diner filled with booths, couples, and families, and they have a menu the size of a phone book. All the booths used to be equipped with phones, just in case you needed to sign a movie deal right then and had to get Creative Artists Agency on the line fast! It was a friendly, unassuming place, your typical Valley delicatessen. Andy ushered me through the doors like he was glued to me, as if we were entering the dark cavern of a smoky bistro instead of the deli entrance near the pie counter. He strode purposefully up to the teenager at the desk and said, "Two for dinner!" It was a commanding performance.

The acne-faced kid at the counter said, "Uh, okay. Sit anywhere you want."

We walked to a booth where Andy adhered to me, all hands on deck, smoothing me into the booth with all eight of his octopus hands. I was befuddled. This new hands-on Lothario *looked* like the same nice guy who just last week had sat patiently across a table from me during a lunch date and never once even tried to initiate a game of footsy. But he was acting like a freak.

We picked up our giant menus and Andy leaned in closely. "Order anything you want, baby, it's on me."

Baby?

Baby?

This was the same fellow who'd spent a half hour on the phone last week describing in detail the wonders of eBay and how men buy more sports memorabilia than women and how well his auctions for rare vinyl were doing. Baby?

There are guys who call you "Baby" and guys who don't. I would have been willing to bet any amount of money that Andy was a guy who had never once in his forty-three years on planet Earth called a woman "Baby" before that night. When he said it, he lowered his voice like a hero in a spaghetti Western, so it was quite a production. It would have been funny if it had been a joke, or ironic, or if he'd been on a bender. But he was still Andy, in a Hawaiian shirt and khaki pants, babying all over the place.

I tried in vain to steer the conversation back into normal territory. I started some nonsense chatter about the traffic, always an excellent go-to subject, and in midsentence he reached over and pushed me into the back of the booth and kissed me. Awkwardly, but with gusto, right over the plate of pickles in the middle of Jerry's Deli.

"Andy," I said. "What on earth has gotten into you? You're acting so . . . different. And I think you got pickle juice on your arm."

"I thought you liked a guy to take charge," he said. "Isn't that what women want?"

"Well, I don't know, maybe, sometimes. But not all at one time," I said. "I liked you just fine the way you were, you know, last week."

And he leaned in again, like he was about to go for Public Torpedo Kiss #2 and at that moment the hand of God interceded in the form of the waitress, who cleared her throat and asked us if we were ready to order.

"Definitely," I said.

And after we'd ordered dinner, I deftly scooted several inches away from Andy and placed my handbag, my hefty heavy handbag, between us like an impenetrable barrier of patent leather. And I did what all nice Southern girls are well trained to do in times like these: tell chatty stories that diffuse the discomfort. And I started with my parents and how I had just talked to them right before our date and they were getting a dog, which reminds me of this one funny story where my brother and I—

"Which brother?" asked Andy.

"Pardon?" I said. Because this being our third date, I hadn't really mentioned I had multiple brothers. Unless perhaps I had mentioned it? Was I hallucinating?

"Was it your brother Guy or your brother Eric?" he asked.

And that was when it dawned on me: Andy had googled me. And he'd found my dorky little blog, a little website I'd thrown together in the depths of my insomnia back in the very beginning days of my divorce, years ago. *Many* years ago. In personal growth years, it was practically ancient history. But judging from his weird behavior, swaggering, "baby"-calling, and uncharacteristic chauvinism, he was reading from the very beginning of my archives back when I thought what I wanted in a man was a scene from a Mae West movie.

Poor Andy! Andy, who thought he had just found the handbook to his brand-new automobile or video game, and he could read this handbook and make adjustments in his steering and maneuvering to get the best performance from his new toy. He was taking notes on me, doing his due diligence, trying to make the engine purr like a cat.

From the way he was swaggering and pushing me into deli booths and attaching his arms to me at all times, I assumed he was somewhere in mid-2005, reading the period of my life known as "trying to figure out what I want from a man now that

I am going to have to date one again." It was a complex and navel-gazing time. I was still deeply interested in revenge fantasies about my ex-husband—fantasies that usually involved me running into Mr. X somewhere when he was alone and sad and wearing mismatched clothes while I was in a size 6 sundress with perfect arms and accompanied by a George Clooney look-alike who was so attracted to me he was draped over me like a sweater.

In these fantasies, which sometimes made it to my stupidly honest online ramblings, I would find a man's man who didn't spend more time on manicures than me or wear more product in his hair than I did, and he would know how to treat a woman. And I think I made up dialogue, because keep in mind, I was in the depths of divorce and also crazy and also drank a lot of merlot. And it all came back to me as I sat there at Jerry's Deli across the table from what had once been a nice Jewish boy from the Valley who drove a station wagon and talked about eBay: I realized with cold certainty that some of my made-up dialogue featured the George Clooney look-alike calling me "baby."

And even though I tried to explain to Andy that all that stuff was just junk I wrote many years ago, he couldn't let it go; he was obsessively interested in my ex-husband and wanted to know why I was so fixated on him.

"I'm not," I said. "I don't think I've even mentioned my ex-husband to you once, other than to say I was divorced."

"But you wrote about him all the time," he said.

"That was years ago! When I was going through my divorce!"

I said. "What . . . did you spend all last night reading the archives? And now you think you know me? And is this why you've suddenly grown six extra hands?"

"Well," he said, defensively. "It's there for anyone to read, and I couldn't stop reading it. And you said you *liked* a guy to call you 'baby.'"

"Oh Lord," I said. And then I flagged down the waitress and canceled my order and asked for another glass of wine.

He felt betrayed by the Internet owner's manual—stupid blog—and our date ended with Andy glowering at me and complaining he had pickle juice on his new Tommy Bahama shirt. He took me home and I never heard from age-appropriate Andy again.

Maybe one day he'll read all the way up to the current year and realize I've outgrown my Rebel Without a Cause of Dissolution days and have evolved into someone who just really wants a nice dinner date with the standard number of hands and no pretend bravado at Jerry's Deli. I don't blame Andy—he thought he'd landed on a gold mine, the intact user's guide for the new software he'd installed. He read the guidebook carefully, making notes, forgetting that women change their minds and their hair color from day to day, not to mention year after year. He'd mistaken Me Version 1.0 (circa 2005) for the present-day Me Version 7.96 beta.

It's all out there, you know. It's on the Internet for anyone in the world to see. Let me serve as a cautionary tale. Either pour out your late-night, near-hysterical personal stories under a pseudonym or decide to date under an assumed name. And if you go the assumed-name route, know in advance your dates will eventually google you, so be sure that your dating pen name isn't the same name used by a mass murderer or reality star. Or a blogger.

Just in case.

Dating in Los Angeles: ~~Like a Yeast Infection, Only Worse~~ Opportunity Calls

After I quit online dating, dating guys who were scandalously young, and dating anyone who knew my real name, the dating pool kind of dried up. It was okay. The end had to come eventually. I didn't know how much longer I could keep complaining.

It ended on a cloudy Thursday evening.

The guy with the earpiece phone arrived twelve minutes late. I had arrived ten minutes early and had already bought myself a cup of coffee (this was my new way of avoiding the embarrassing and potentially date-ending moment when the male portion of the date stands with you in line and you both order coffee and then you both reach the register and it's the stupid, ceaselessly awkward moment of who will pay. And if he doesn't want to buy me a piddly cup of coffee, I know already the date is certain to go downhill from there. It's two lousy bucks! . . . And even though I realize how Victorian and Scarlett O'Hara and old-fashioned this sounds, I don't even care anymore. So now I arrive early and buy my own damn coffee, thereby avoiding this pitfall).

He hadn't been Guy with the Earpiece Phone when I met him. He sat next to me on the subway, and at that time, he was Guy Sitting Beside Me. I always take the subway instead of the bus on rainy days. While the subway is infinitely more grotesque than the commuter bus, it at least doesn't have to sit in rainy-day traffic on the Hollywood Freeway for two and a half hours each way.

The rain had started in the middle of the night, and I woke up to a noise, a strange foreign noise. Was it some rattling truck going by? A stealth helicopter pattering above the house? I lifted the blinds and saw the raindrops on the windowpane. "Oh, wow! Rain."

You know you have lived in Los Angeles too long when you can't discern the noise of rain.

Then, "Oh crud. Rain. Traffic will be unbearable."

Los Angeles steals away your love of a rainy day through its powers of gridlock. I remember lying in my bed during one long Mississippi summer during my freshman year of college when it rained so much the houseplants began to mold, and I loved each rainy afternoon because there was nothing that had to be done, just reading books, listening to Joni Mitchell albums, and waiting for a big thunderstorm to knock out all the lights. It rains so much in the Southeast that it's just part of life, and people don't freak out and run into guardrails at the sight of mist.

Here in the bright lights of Hollyweird, it rains about six days a year. It always seems to start two hours before rush-hour traffic on a Monday morning. The top news story is "Storm Watch! Will We All Perish?" and TV reporters in slickers stand out by overpasses and near puddles in Sherman Oaks doing man-on-the-street interviews of poor, wet Los Angelenos who've braved the rain for a morning latte.

Traffic instantly comes to a standstill the moment the first raindrop lands upon the first windshield. It's a complex ballet of fender benders and skidding big rigs and cars leaping over guardrails. You'd never guess that all it takes to bring the second-largest city in America to its knees is the gentle patter of mist.

And so on rainy days I gird myself against the elements and brave the perma-sweat smell of the subway. The subway in Los Angeles is unique in that it goes virtually nowhere, is used entirely on the honor system with no turnstiles or ticket-takers, and is the underground home of the homeless and disturbed. I once saw a woman completely disrobe in the Universal City underground station. It was remarkable how she danced her way out of her urine-soaked clothes, and all around commuters in suits and ties, hospital scrubs, and chef's whites ignored her, as if she didn't exist at all.

On the morning I met Guy Sitting Beside Me, I was wearing waterproof boots and quietly reading *How to Practice: The Way to A Meaningful Life* by His Holiness the Dalai Lama. I was rereading the chapter on aspiring to enlightenment, as just that morning I had managed to share the California state bird with at least seven people in traffic on the way to the subway station and honk at yet four more drivers.

He sat down next to me and was silent too, until the next

stop, when he asked me what I was reading. I held up the front cover of the book, expecting that the smiley face and Buddha-like pose of the Dalai Lama on the cover would cease further conversation, but he surprised me.

"Hey, the Dalai Lama," he said. "Cool."

And we spent the next five segments of the Red Line talking about the rain, the crappy traffic, and where each of us work downtown. And that's when he asked me if I wanted to meet for coffee after work. He was cute and hadn't automatically assumed I was a bank teller just because I work at a bank (why is it that when you tell someone you work at a bank they always ask if you're a teller? Is that the only job women are allowed to have at banks? Is this 1955?). So I said yes.

But when he arrived twelve minutes late for our date, he was Guy with the Earpiece Phone. He had the ear thingamajig clipped to his head and a little blue light flashed intermittently. He saw me and waved and came over to where I had staked out a table.

"Sorry I'm late," he said. "Rain." And then he went up to order a coffee and sat back down again and we started talking. All first-date chitchat is sort of nerve-racking, but it seemed to be going okay.

He asked me a question about my job, and I was responding when, in the middle of my sentence, he said, "Hey, I'm having coffee," which was weird, because I was there and I knew he was having coffee, as I could clearly see both his hands and his coffee cup right there in front of me.

"So, anyway . . ." I said.

"Hey, hang on just a minute," he said.

So I paused.

"I just have to take this call," he said. Then I guess he noticed the blank stare on my face, so he pointed to his earpiece phone doodad, which is when it dawned on me that he had already taken the call midway through me talking and was connected via earpiece to someone else and letting the caller, not me, know of his coffee whereabouts. I couldn't tell which one of us should be more embarrassed—him for being so rude or me for not realizing he'd been talking to someone else. So I just sat quietly while he finished his call.

"Hey, sorry about that," he said. "So what were you saying?"

And I took a sip of coffee and decided to pretend that the weird thing had never happened, and we started chatting again. Then it happened again! This time while he was talking, he interrupted himself and took another call. And then another call.

It was impressive, actually. It was just like being on the phone with someone while you tell them this awful/embarrassing/troubling thing that happened and you realize they are only half listening to you while they surf the Web or check e-mail. Sometimes you can hear them typing.

"You know, if this is a bad time, I really understand," I said. "I mean, I have to leave pretty soon anyway."

"Oh no," he said. "It's not a bad time. I just had to take that call."

When I say "I have to take this call," it is because my house might be on fire or someone has died. His urgent calls that couldn't wait twenty minutes seemed to be about fantasy football, someone's plans for later that night, and, if I overheard correctly, someone calling to say they would text him later.

And just then he needed to take another call. So while he was drinking coffee and carrying on a one-sided conversation with his goofy earpiece, I picked up my cell phone and opened it up and answered a fake call of my own.

"Really? No way! Yeah, I can be right there!" I said. I snapped my cell phone shut, stood up, and grabbed my purse and jacket.

"Hang on a sec," said Earpiece Guy to caller number eleventeen. "You gotta run?" he asked me.

"Yeah," I said, shaking my head. "Really sorry about this, that was a friend of mine. She's having car trouble, so I'm going to go pick her up. Anyway, great seeing you!"

"Oh, okay," he said. "Give me a call sometime!"

Of course. I'll be sure to do that.

An Inconvenient Truth

It's lunchtime and my friend and coworker Corey and I are sitting in the corporate lunchroom knitting. People in businessy button-down shirts and ties look over at us occasionally, because knitting might be construed as fun, or merrymaking, or even wasting time, and as such is very out of character in the corporate lunchroom.

"Do you think dating is different in other places?" I ask her. "Do you think there are other parts of the country where the goods aren't so . . . in desperate need of therapy?"

"Oh! Come on!" she says. "Dating is fun!"

"You've been married for what? Twelve years?" My face is

pinched. I can feel it pinching. This is what happens when people who don't have to date in Los Angeles give me advice or words of encouragement about dating. I pucker up like I've swallowed a whole lemon.

"Only married people think dating is fun," I tell her. "You have a sweet nostalgic notion that dating is happy and charming, and fluttery first-date feeling. In real life, this is Los Angeles, and dating is like playing Russian roulette with humans. You could meet a nice guy who doesn't want to tie you up (much), or you could meet that crazy guy who secretly posts ads on Craigslist looking for a woman to pee on him."

"Okay," she said. "Maybe I have been out of the game for a few years. But I don't think it's any better in other cities. In L.A. it's probably just easier to meet a wider variety of crazy people."

Dating isn't *fun*. It's not always awful, mind you, and sometimes your date will do something unexpected and lovely, like open the door for you and pretend that he likes cats. But the most valuable reason to embark upon a dating spree is for the wisdom—and the great stories. The truth is, I have learned so much about myself and so many life lessons from dating. For example, I've learned that it's a very bad idea to casually date anyone who works at one of your favorite stores or who is in any way connected to the mechanics of your daily life, like the cute produce guy at the grocery store or the bus driver with the great arms. Because, unless you can be absolutely 100 percent certain that you are never breaking up, you will either find yourself shopping at an inconvenient grocery store with bad lighting or, in the case of Mr. Nice Arms, you'll be driving to work for the next three months until the bus drivers all change shifts again.

I decided to cheer myself up and make a list of all the great growth-enhancement opportunities that have come as a result of dating in Los Angeles.

What I Have Learned About Myself as a Person from Dating Freaks in Los Angeles

1. No matter where I live, I will always be a Southern girl and expect men to have manners.

2. Manners are truly nearly extinct.

3. If someone invites me out to something, even though I really do want to try to be all liberal-minded and easygoing and not a judgmental, mean sort of person (since men have a way of twisting this around and making you feel all latently Stepford or golddiggery for thinking so), I am just going to admit out loud on paper right now for the record that I still think it is tacky to invite me to coffee or lunch or dinner and then ask me to split the bill. ESPECIALLY IF IT IS UNDER TEN BUCKS!!!!!!! Pony up the stupid ten bucks! It is not that I can't afford to pay for my own sandwich. It is not that I need a man to feed me and clothe me and provide a roof over my head. It is for the simple generosity of spirit and the basic premise of dating! When did people start thinking it was more romantic to split the bill? Have people lost their damn minds?

4. If the male portion of the date takes a call during our date, it better be because someone died. Or because their

car is being towed. Those are the only two acceptable reasons.

5. After personal discovery and some trial and error, I have learned with great certainty that men who text a girl at midnight with "what's up?" are not interested in your sparkling personality, your view of the world economy, your great jokes, or even your ability to enjoy action movies. THEY JUST WANT TO MATTRESS MAMBO.

6. While I have taken on my life as an art project and have even written entire lists of goals on how to improve myself, I am not some guy's fixer-upper. If they want a handyman's special, they can look elsewhere. (See: Man who argued with me, a woman, about the existence of the G-spot.) Just because a guy can't find it doesn't mean it isn't there.

7. There are some funny people out there.

8. Men who say, "You have HOW MANY cats?" should be immediately informed you have only three cats—but seven children, all under the age of nine. Won't you be their new daddy?

9. Don't give up and lower your standards. There is nobody on the planet worth your self-worth. Set the bar high and someone somewhere will rise up to meet it.

10. Eventually.

I Came, I Saw, I Decided Not to Rush It

Sometimes I get a notion in my head—for example, like

single women my age are expected to be dating and living it up—and I work at it like it's a class I've signed up for and I'm being graded on the final result. This makes me appear to be a type A personality, a real go-getter who makes a goal and reaches for it enthusiastically. I'm more of a type A-minus, really. I decide on some activity, goal, or hairstyle and commit to it, and when it runs its course, or when I embarrass myself to the extent that I have to leave town, I mark the item off my mental to-do list with a sigh of relief.

Four months was about the limit to my crash course in self-mandated summer dating. My annual report will note that fact. ("In the second quarter of the year, she dated. Next quarter we expect to see high returns on her commitment to manicures.") Not all the dates I went on were bad or ridiculous, but the moderately pleasant dates and the comfortably nice ones aren't very interesting to write about. Also, I've run out of pseudonyms, and fear I might accidentally name a real person.

Like vacations and meals, the dates that go all wrong or end up with someone calling the law are always the ones you remember. The few nice guys I met were usually looking to settle down, and I would try diligently to picture myself in a relationship again, or envision us going on vacation together, and I just couldn't see it. It all looked vague and hazy and a little stifling.

I would start feeling antsy and nervous, asking myself things like, *Will I have to do his laundry? Will I have to start cooking for him? What if he's clingy? What if he snores? But why do I have to meet all his friends and pretend I like them? I already have friends.* It became obvious that I was just not there yet, not at the settle-down-and-nest chapter in my life story. I was settled down for so long—and before that, wishing to be settled down—that now I start looking for exit doors on the third date, memorizing escape routes in case he invites me to a family event or tries to get both my home number *and* my cell number. Horrifyingly enough, I seem to have turned into a stereotypical guy. If I start talking about football during a funeral, someone call my parents and tell them to come fetch me and get me out of this heathen, corrupted city.

Is it a myth that all single women in the entire universe desperately long for a stable, committed relationship? All the self-help books I've read, and I still don't know any of the answers; it's a travesty. Most of my examples about life come from trashy books, movies, and the TV. According to all the hours I have watched and read about American relationships, I should be married to some overweight guy who can't remember our anniversary, and when he gives me a singing plastic fish as a gift, I should roll my eyes and canned applause should fill the living room. Either that or a team of unusually good-looking crime scene detectives should be inspecting my bathroom with a blue light.

In the movies, single women my age are desperate, pathetic, and poorly dressed—or evil megalomaniacs who abuse their cute assistants. Having even one cat defines a typical on-screen character as a spinster, and only after a montage and a makeover can she catch the eye of the leading man. I'm not the only one who knows about the typecast crazy cat lady. I've seen the cautiously raised eyebrow as soon as a prospective date learns I have a cat. Telling them I have three cats really thins out the crowd. But I don't *feel* like a crazy cat lady. And what about the crazy dog ladies? How come no one ever talks about them or compares them to the creeping crotch funk of insanity?

A single woman can have a giant sixty-pound dog and no one makes jokes or snide comments about it. But if you have three cats, each weighing about twelve-ish pounds and totaling far less than the body weight of one dog, people begin to lump you in with the homeless, the crackpots, and the mentally unstable. There are real personal ads online where men specifically state that the woman of his dreams must own no cats, almost like he's looking for an apartment. ("In search of small, well-maintained girl with a short lease. No cats allowed.")

After my initial spree of dating, I stopped working at it like it was a graded homework assignment. It was a relief to settle back into life and close my online dating account and start going to the grocery store in faded yoga pants and flip-flops again. I felt the same way about it that I do about saving leftovers: that I am doing something necessary and good. And then, four months later when I throw them out, I feel good all over again for doing something necessary and probably lifesaving.

One day when I'm ready to meet someone who doesn't immediately make me look for the nearest exit, I assume I'll have my own montage scene and canned audience applause, and then I will make jokes about him adopting my cats and we'll buy a riding lawn mower. I'll tell stories about all the time I spent being a twentysomething guy while I was in my late thirties. Until then, I'll be working on the rest of my to-do list. The last quarter of the year is looking good for another vacation alone, this time with a big stack of glossy magazines for the plane ride and some drippy mystery to read on a beach.

Roll the credits, end the chapter. Add applause.

Crazy Adjacent Zucchini

I love that my real address is not actually in Encino, California, but is Encino Adjacent, as if that were a real place. And yet in Los Angeles it is perfectly acceptable to tell people you live in Encino Adjacent, because people get it. They are, after all, living in Sherman Oaks Adjacent, Beverly Hills Adjacent, or Hollywood Hills Adjacent.

I think about moving every few months, usually after a long day's commute, but then I come home to the sounds of my neighbors to the left having a backyard boogie with a piñata, while my neighbors directly behind me are playing the sound track to *Hair* and loudly discussing their dog's new agent. Really. Their dog has an agent. And I looked around my yard and decided, once and for all again, to stay at my house for just a little while longer because I have become completely and totally obsessed with growing a square watermelon, and to achieve this goal, I must have a place to grow said watermelon—such as a backyard.

It all began innocently enough. Earlier in the day I was having lunch with three of my coworkers, and one of the guys at the table was telling me about his most recent trip to Japan and about the expensive cantaloupe he'd eaten there.

"How expensive is 'expensive' in melon dollars?" I asked.

"It was about a hundred dollars for the cantaloupe," he said.

"For how many cantaloupes?" I asked. "How much cantaloupe can one person eat on vacation?"

"Oh, it was just one," he said. "One hundred dollars for one cantaloupe."

I stared at him for a minute.

"Did you feel really dumb after you bought a hundred-dollar cantaloupe?" I asked.

Then my other coworker chimed in. "Was it square?"

I turned to look at her in astonishment. "Now that's normally the sort of ridiculous question I ask! I've rubbed off on you!" I said.

She laughed. "No, seriously, they do have square watermelons in Japan, you know."

"They do not!" I said. "Stop fibbing. This is just like the time you told me that all cell phones have a GPS locator in them!"

And in unison—and also disgust—they said, "They do."

So, of course, after lunch we all returned to Corporate Job, Inc. and focused on the important and dedicated task of researching the existence of square watermelons. And happily, I was wrong, because they do exist, and I found pictures on the Internet that looked real enough to make me believe in these square, green watermelons.

I discussed with every engineer at work the possible growing and shaping container options, what the building materials may be, and what will be hinged or removable, and then decided to set out on a path of science and also, probably, drunkenness, because nothing goes better with gardening and mad science experiments than a nice, cold beer. And I am going to transform my backyard into a growing wonderland of square fruit.

I feel I may have finally found my life's calling: drinking beer and writing about failed attempts at gardening. Because already this little adventure of mine is starting out on the crazy foot, and I have yet to plant even a single seed.

Exhibit A: My Gardener Laughs at Me

One of the interesting quirks about people in Los Angeles is that none of them do their own yard work. No one mows their own yard (no one washes their own car, either, but that's a whole different story), and so my little rented piddlysquat house comes with a gardener. The landlord deals with all the particulars, and it's included in my rent, so once a week someone comes and blows the leaves around. This is standard procedure at every house in my neighborhood. At first I thought it was strange that no one maintained their own lawn, but after a while it just fades into the normal routine of living in this weird city.

The first gardener was dark-eyed and quiet and lasted a few months. I have no idea what happened to him. A few weeks later the new gardener appeared, and his name is Francisco. He's friendly and talkative and sometimes brings his son along to help blow the dirt and leaves around.

Francisco and I have talked about my desire to create a garden, and also how I don't want to cut off my foot with a rototiller while digging up the backyard. He suggested creating raised beds for the garden and offered to bring me some scrap lumber and dirt, which he will sell to me for "*muy* cheap."

"Okay," I said. "So we're all set on the dirt? Next Saturday you'll bring it by?"

"*Sí,*" said Francisco. "*El fin de semana.* Okay?"

"Thanks, sounds great!" I said. "Oh! Francisco? Is it organic dirt?"

He paused. It was a very long pause.

"*Sí,*" he said, finally. "Sure, miss . . . *es organic* dirt."

And we looked at each other for one long moment while Francisco studiously tried not to burst out laughing. Then I walked inside, and as I closed the door, I heard his son say, "*organic* dirt!" and they had a hearty little chuckle. *Organic dirt! Qué loco!*

I can only imagine the conversation that Francisco will have repeatedly with other gardeners in the Greater Los Angeles and North Valley region. And the laughter. Oh, the laughter!

And then this crazy-ass white lady asked me if the dirt *was* organic!!

Gardeners from across the city will laugh and then tell him, "You should charge her more for it! Crazy lady and her *organic dirt!*" And to Francisco, and to all gardeners who have heard the tale of the Crazy White Woman and Her Organic Dirt, all I have to say is, wait until you see the way I grow a watermelon!

Lo, So Begins the Garden of Eatin'

My house has two backyards. There is the normal backyard that stretches off the patio about seven feet deep, with some grass, a couple of trees, and an overgrown geranium bush in the corner. At the back of this backyard is a giant hedge that reaches more than nine feet tall and spreads out about twelve feet wide, and behind this hedge lies what I fondly call the Back Forty. It is the back backyard.

I have no idea what kind of loopy person back in 1942 decided it would be a great idea to grow a hedge in the middle of the yard, separating it into two yards. My friends have various theories. One suggested that it may have been a way for the original homeowners to disguise untidy yard things, or maybe laundry, or both. But apparently 1940s-era loopy found its 2000-era perfect match, because I love the hedge divider. It gives me a secret garden in the Back Forty, plus provides a much cozier atmosphere in the front backyard.

Before I decided to embark upon my new path of growing square fruit, my back backyard was a vast, empty wasteland of nothingness. The soil is hard and mostly clay, and I shut off the Back Forty sprinklers months ago, so the few weeds shriveled up or wandered off to someone else's better-maintained real yard. The goal was to kill off the weeds and remaining straggly grass so it would be easier to dig up come planting time. I planned to create two raised beds (shallow, but still raised), fill them with dirt, and let the magic begin.

One Saturday, I began my Great Gardening Adventure by heading to the Back Forty to size up potential placement for the raised beds. I looked at the bare ground and the dry weeds and pronounced it a fine and decent home for my future field of dreams. Then I got into the car and went shopping.

The first step to any successful venture is shopping. I made the rounds that day—garden supply centers, Target, Walmart, and finally Home Depot. I should interject here that I had no actual building plans, sketches, measurements, or details for my raised garden beds. Francisco had not come through yet on either the dirt or the building supplies, so I walked the aisles of each store looking for mulch, hinges, plywood, and whatever struck my fancy. My dream of a square watermelon patch was self-sustaining; dreamers like me can't be bothered with little details like "How long is this thing?" and also "What is it made of?" and "How much will this cost me?"

I purchased my supplies and went home, determined to have a nice glass of cabernet and build the beginning of the Greatest Garden Ever Made. In just a few quick hours, about six and a half, I managed to get four pieces of lumber nailed together and created the first frame of what I was sure would be my master-piece. It was a little lopsided and slightly longer on one end than the other. I stood back, raised my glass, admired my work, and waited for my organic dirt to arrive.

The Gardener Wants a Divorce

Francisco and I are standing in the backyard. Neither of us has said a word to the other for a full five minutes. He is leaning on his shovel and staring at me, and he is angry, or frustrated, or both. I had planned to tell him all about my exciting square watermelon patch, but now we aren't speaking. We need therapy or couples counseling. I suspect he wants to divorce me on the grounds of insanity.

Aside from the fact that we do not live under the same roof, and I don't do his dirty laundry, Francisco and I are in a marriage. We don't talk much, we both share the responsibility for the upkeep of the yard, and sometimes we don't listen to each other or understand each other. Sometimes we laugh or have a beer, but we never have s-e-x.

Sounds like marriage to me.

Francisco finally brought a big pile of bagged dirt over and dropped it outside the garage. That's as far as we've gotten, because he wants to trim the big hedges today, and I am trying to convince him otherwise. He has a vision for the shrubs that I do not share, and every time he stops by, it seems something has been removed or cut to within an inch of its life. There used to be big box shrubs in front of the house. One day I came home to find them carved into trees. Now I make jokes to my friends: "Ya'll come over! Look at the shrubs! You can't see the forest because of the tiny, stubby trees!"

On this particular day, however, I have mortally offended Francisco. Our relationship is on the rocks. I have made the egregious error of implying that he killed the big backyard oak tree when he completely chopped it to pieces, or "pruned" it a few months ago.

"Francisco, I'm sorry. I'm sure you didn't kill the tree; it just died coincidentally around the same time, maybe?"

"It's not dead," he says.

"But it has no branches and no leaves."

"Look!" he says impatiently. He gestures to a stubby branch. "Right here, *es verde*, okay?"

"Okay. But this one green leaf bud will not shade me for the whole summer. If you cut down the hedges, too, I'll bake over here. This is the Valley. It gets *hot*."

"Bake?"

It occurs to me that maybe the only way to appeal to Francisco on this issue is to make him understand that while his idea is surely really great, and I was so, so wrong to imply he killed the tree, I have special needs, and they are girly and silly, but I would be so happy if he would oblige me. Being married taught me a thing or two about the fragile male ego.

So I change my tone.

"Francisco, I know you're right about the hedges. I do! But this is a little embarrassing, you know? I'm . . . very pale-colored. And without any shade, I'll get sunburned, and I'll be bright red and super ugly. And, you know, I just don't want to be red and ugly. I need some shade, that's all, even though you are completely right about the hedges . . ."

He hesitates.

He looks at the hedge. Looks back at me, as if discovering for the first time that I really do glow in the dark, probably, and while he doesn't find the shade of a giant hedge very pleasant, perhaps this loco lady has challenges he had not considered.

"Well," he says slowly, taking his time. "Okay. No cutting hedges today."

"Thank you, Francisco!" I hug the gardener. We're both relieved. Neither of us really wants to divorce each other. Yet.

Francisco finishes with the grass, and I sweep the patio, and then we have a beer and I decide that today is maybe not the best day to tell him about the square watermelons after all. I don't even push him to carry all that dirt to the back backyard. It would just lead to more misunderstandings, more distance between us, and Lord knows I cannot afford couples counseling for me and the gardener.

Gardening, Week Three: An Intervention, or Perhaps Prozac, Is Necessary

A few days after the narrowly averted hedge destruction, I came home to find the only pretty thing in the entire backyard hacked up and sheared off. It used to be a huge flowering geranium that had probably been planted when the house was built and over time had expanded to cover the bare, ugly concrete wall dividing my yard from the neighbor's yard. There was barely anything left of it. Francisco had kept the hedge intact but exacted his revenge on the flowers. One wonders what the gardener's own yard must look like. A barren wasteland of stubby shrubs and hacked-up trees? One tries not to envision it. One drinks a glass of wine the size of one's own head and mourns the loss of the pretty flowers.

Finally, I call my landlord.

"Francisco is nice and all, but he needs medication."

The landlord sighs. "I'll see what I can do," he said. "He seems to be on a mission, doesn't he?"

I agreed. "The tree is still dead from his pruning adventure."

"Francisco works on the yard at my house, too," said the land-lord, "and one day last week he pulled out all of my wife's decorative grasses. She almost had a heart attack."

"Perhaps he's missed his calling as a lumberjack," I said. "Or butcher. Ax-wielding maniac?"

My landlord tells me, voice lowered, "My wife almost left me when she saw the bougainvillea at the back of our house. It has four leaves left on it."

Pause. Take a sip. It has become quite clear: between myself and the landlord, neither of us has any balls.

"Why are you and I such pushovers?" I ask. "Why do we let Francisco run our lives?"

"He's the one with the electric shears; that's my guess." Then we grumble and toast to nature in its bounty, with its amazing ability to grow back.

We hope.

This Burns Calories, Right?

Finally I gave up the hope that Francisco would help me haul all the dirt to the back of the yard, and now I am hobbled over and limping. I have apparently suffered a gardening-related injury. I am so pitifully out of shape that hauling a few bags of dirt around has crippled me.

I should probably use my treadmill more often or do some sport besides knitting.

I didn't even haul around that much garden-related stuff. In fact, I carried one or two bags of mulch, and the rest of the lifting and "put it here . . . no . . . over there . . . let's move this, too!"

was carried out by two very nice men who had the dire misfortune to be working on a house directly next to me.

The house next door to me, previously rented by Mark and Sherri, a very nice couple, is now being put up for sale, and for the past couple of weeks all sorts of hammering and drilling and painting has been going on over there. I have just been ignoring it, since I know that with my luck the folks who buy that house will be either (a) loud talkers/yellers/all-night partyers, (b) super quiet people who despise my breathing noise, (c) Satan worshippers who make live pigeon sacrifices in the backyard, or (d) drug dealers. So, I have just ignored the whole house-is-for-sale-to-possible-Satanists aspect. However, on Saturday morning I was introduced to Octavio and Julio, both of whom were very sorry to bother me, but could I please come outside?

Not a good sign, usually.

They had apparently been sawing down the tree that sits between my yard and the neighbor's yard when a large chunk of the tree crashed into my back patio. So I went outside with Octavio and Julio, and we looked at my backyard and the large tree that was covering much of my patio.

"Shady!" I said.

"Accidental!" they said.

"Is it too early for a beer?" asked guess who.

"Never too early!" said Octavio.

And after much chitchatting and scrutinizing of the downed soldier, everyone decided perhaps the best thing to do would be to push it back over the fence to the other side. Mind you, I had nothing to do with this flash of brilliance, as I was doing the thing that all good Southerners do when faced with a tree spontaneously committing suicide over their back porch: I was opening up cold beers and hostessing. Because this is what nice Southern girls do even when they are long past being both nice and anywhere in the age range of girlish. I can't chainsaw a tree or haul it off to the . . . tree place, or whatever people do with giant pieces of greenery. But I can facilitate and hostess and make small talk.

After twenty minutes of trying to push a giant tree back into the yard from whence it came, everyone was ready for another round, and Octavio and Julio decided perhaps, with my permission, they would just saw it here and carry it off piece by piece?

And as day turned into evening turned into six-pack and the tree left little by little, I realized that the Almighty himself had sent me these two new best buddies, and they felt so bad about a tree landing on my porch that they would agree to do anything, and also they were maybe a little intoxicated. And I had eleventeen hundred pounds of potting soil in giant bags just waiting for someone to haul to the future site of my watermelon patch. And I had procrastinated for about as long as one can procrastinate when they are on a square watermeloning craze, and the dirt needed to make it to the Back Forty for the transplanting, and I had found two poor schmoes to help me haul eleventeen hundred pounds of potting soil on Sunday. If a tree falls in Encino Adjacent, will Scarlett O'Hara think about her garden the next day? Indeed!

During the Great Dirt Distribution Project of 2006, I carried enough mulch to wake up in the morning hobbled and aching, and then I lied to everyone at work and said I was hunched over and crippled from a weekend of extreme hanky-panky, which I am sure they really believed, especially after one person suggested I downgrade to a "battery-operated model."

The Garden of Constant Sorrow

Planting is more fun than hauling dirt. After the soil was scattered into the raised-bed garden boxes, I arranged each watermelon seedling neatly in a corner and filled the rest of the space with little flowers, some herbs, and a single zucchini seedling. The mulch was mulchified, the seedlings were settled in, and I stared at my garden, willing it to grow.

And then the heat wave came.

Dante's Seventh Circle of Hell is located in the center of my backyard. It is kind of brown and twiggy and is surprisingly close to multiple 7-11 stores and gas stations and one very good Persian grocery store.

It's not enough that everything died during the heat wave—the watermelons, the peppers, the basil—and it wasn't from lack of water (I watered as often as I could without drowning everything); the plants simply burned. The leaves had actual burn marks from the scorching sun. Nothing could take twenty straight days of 109 to 118 degrees Fahrenheit except the succulents and desert plants.

I made my peace with it and said, "Woo-hoo! Look at how big that cactus has gotten!" My cactus loves the heat, and so I love it. From afar, of course.

With the weather cooling down, however, I was sure the worst was over. Marine layer! Temps in the high eighties! Maybe stuff will grow again where once there was grass. Life regains a glimmer of hope.

The hedges had survived the heat wave but not Francisco. They were left unguarded as I threw caution to the wind and ran errands instead of holding fast and firm as the protector of all that remains green and alive in my yard. Francisco got his way after all.

A Tale of Two Gardeners

I had a dream—I had an awesome dream—that one day I would see square watermelons sitting side-by-side with round ones, that actual vegetables would spring forth from my garden, that visible panty lines could be abolished forever, which has nothing to do with gardening but is, alas, still a dream.

And then, you know, I kind of woke up and was like, "Holy crap! It's hot outside and there are ants!" So I had a cocktail and sat indoors and watched *Midnight in the Garden of Good and Evil,* which, frankly, is about as close as I got to gardening after the great heat wave.

Somewhere between the great drought and the great pruning—and, oh, more pruning and a tree falling on my yard—I guess the square watermelon dream died. Nice knowing you, seedlings! Sorry about the 118-degree summer! Blame it all on the hole in the ozone, probably from the hair spray I used in my formative teenage years, much needed to achieve the impenetrable Wall O' Bangs.

So, the backyard had been looking kind of sad. And so did the front yard, because Francisco had stopped coming so frequently. I saw him in August and he said, "Ah, no really need to cut the back today; it's all dead anyway." That statement grew into his overarching philosophy, I suppose. Prune and hack and remove, ergo, making the job of gardener almost totally work free! Fabuloso!

Francisco thought he had the situation at Chez Brown Yard pretty well tied up. *Nice loco white lady with her organic dirt (Ha! Ha! Organic dirt!) and her crazytalk of watermelon with squares. Who knows! Beer!* Things were good for Francisco.

But then things changed. An interloper tried to steal the crazy lady away, and *Francisco get very mad.* It all happened innocently enough. I was coming home from visiting Grandma in Orange County one Sunday afternoon, piling out of my Jeep and generally trying to Sherpa my way to the house with all my bags, when from out of nowhere *(where did he come from?),* a very cute guy offered to help me carry things up to my porch.

Normal people would say "No!" This is a crime-infested urban center, after all. We have psychotic madmen roaming the streets at all times. But I handed him three more bags of stuff and he helped me lug it all to the patio. He did not, it turns out, mystically appear out of nowhere. He and his father have a landscaping service and tree-trimming business, and would I be looking for the services of a very good gardener?

"Because your yard," he said, ". . . it is not so much pretty."

"Thank you," I said. "My gardener has a strategy, I think. He's really into conserving water, maybe?"

"Ahhh," said the serious young man with the very nice dimple. He was quiet for a minute. He looked at my garden, then looked at me. "*Todo está muerto.*"

"*Sí,*" I said. "*Todo está muerto.*" Everything is dead. Cue the sad music, roll credits, and pass the tequila.

Somehow, somewhere, the United Gardener Interpersonal Communication system must have been triggered. Just the mere presence of another gardener—a rival, at that—standing on my front lawn and chitchatting about crabgrass sparked a psychic flurry of competition, or something, because Francisco, whom I had not seen in three weeks, instantly showed up in his truck with his leaf blower at the ready.

He eyed the interloper.

"*Quién es* this guy?" said Francisco.

"Oh, I didn't get his name," I said. Then I turned to Mystery Landscape Guy. "So, what is your name?"

"I am Abel." (I admit it took me a minute. I was like, "You're able? Able to do what?" because . . . I am not so fast sometimes.)

So there was a pause. And then it sunk in . . . his name was Abel, and he was . . . able! This is how I think, and it amused me. So I giggled, which didn't do much to break the tension at El Muerto Yard.

Francisco eyed Abel. Abel eyed me.

I eyed my cuticles with great interest. Then I looked at Francisco, and he looked so sad. Like that time in fifth grade when I broke up with Kevin Anderson for not holding my hand on the bus. So I turned to Abel and said, "Well, nice to meet you! This is Francisco, my gardener. I gotta go!" Francisco smiled with what was either relief or indigestion, and, coward that I am, I locked myself inside with my herd of cats and nothing that even vaguely resembled the great outdoors.

But since then, Francisco has been coming every week, and my yard is only a little bit *muerto*. I guess some healthy competition is good for all men. Even those who really, really prefer to cut and run.

And Then There Were Squash

According to weather news, this is the longest dry spell Los Angeles has experienced in 130 years. I'm wary of the fire season; last year and the year before were too close for comfort. This year I have even more to protect from the scorching heat and fire danger, however.

This year I finally have plants.

The raised-bed garden I built as part of the Failed Square Watermelon Project sat there for a good amount of time, all sad and empty after my tiny watermelon seedlings burned up in solid week of one-thousand degree Valley weather. It is now home to *twelve* little squash seedlings, because squash is a warm-weather plant and allegedly loves the sun. The wildfire, not so much. But sun is supposed to be good for squash.

Having been a renter for so many years, I have always been a container gardener, and I usually have pretty good success in the containers. So in addition to the raised bed I built, there are big plastic and pottery containers all over the backyard. I've had some of these pots for ten, twelve years now. Most of them held giant cacti and succulents. But the first winter I lived in this

house, the winter when I got divorced and insane and not neces-
sarily in that order, we had a hard frost and almost everything
died. I was sad at first, but then it felt kind of good to make a
clean start. I often forget that things and possessions and even
plants carry energy and memories. Now I don't look out on the
patio and see plants I had in a married house from way back
when; I see a whole bunch of new happy little faces and just one
or two old friends.

One weekend my friend Faith and I wandered the aisles of
the Green Thumb nursery in Canoga Park, looking at their
lovely herb selection and picking up each happily potted plant
and smelling them, touching the leaves, and at some point I
believe I even hugged a culinary-grade French rosemary. I
bought apple mint, three varieties of thyme, the aforementioned
rosemary, Greek oregano, cilantro, and basil.

Most of my plants sit on little wheeled plant stands so I can
move them into the shade when the next Big Heat Wave arrives.
I did not install a drip irrigation system because it was too expensive, and I had already spent my entire budget on plants and potting soil and so on. But I cleaned the patio and arranged
everything so that I could just buy one of those special nozzles
for the garden hose that simulate rainwater, and I'm going to
hose the patio down at night when I water the plants, which I
hope will have the added benefit of keeping Spider City at a
more manageable level (the amount of dust, leaves, dirt, and cob-
webs on the patio was rather startling. Apparently I was very
busy last year and did not have time for such pursuits as sweeping and noticing the debris).

The plants are still green. This must be a gardening world record! Already now it's been two, three weeks and nothing has died—everything else is actually alive and growing. It's not a coincidence; it's got to be a collective sigh of relief on the part of my poor plants.

The landlord fired Francisco. It took the landlord's wife threatening to move out after what I hear was a particularly tragic incident involving her Meyer Lemon tree, but one day Francisco was let go, and I felt a little sad until I noticed that the hedges began to sprout new growth, the geranium flowered, and even the tree out back has sensed the departure of Francisco and has started to show leaves! After its terrifying near-death prune, I'm surprised to see it make the effort, but somehow nature has sensed the disappearance of Francisco and made a valiant effort to regroup and regrow.

One of the new gardeners came by yesterday after work, and I showed him the Back Forty and gave him the key to the gate. He is about sixty and tanned smooth brown from working outside, and he's very businesslike and gave a quick assessment of the trimming work Francisco had done.

"This guy was not knowing anything," he said very seriously. Gravely. He looked at the shrubs in front and sighed so deeply I knew he could feel those damn hedges hurting, in pain. I just thought they were funny, my little forest of stunted trees shaped by madness and half dead from neglect. The new gardeners are very serious and more than a little intimidating. They lectured me about the ivy problem. I didn't even realize I had an ivy problem.

The head honcho gardener is named Juan and he brought his assistants along for the walk-through, and they politely endured me as I bragged about my containers and my raised bed full of rapidly growing zucchini. I didn't know the Spanish word for it, so I told him he'd just have to wait and see. Juan looked at my plants skeptically and mostly ignored me. I made a mental note to ask the engineers at work if they thought I might be able to create a contraption that would turn all my zucchinis square. Just for fun.

Where the Big Things Grow

While other things in the garden mysteriously mutated, died, and passed on through the karmic vegetation loop, as summer moved into fall, my backyard began sprouting forth with giant, formidable gadzukes.

My little half-dead zucchini plants turned into a plush forest of squash. And they just kept coming! Nothing stopped them, not even my mysterious watering regimen. I left town for a few days, and what had once been a teensy little four-inch zuke grew and morphed into a Loch Ness Zucchinister! I weighed one of them in the bathroom, and it tipped the scale at seventeen pounds. I grew a seventeen-pound zucchini! It is truly a miracle.

So I do hereby declare I am pretty much not going to plant anything ever again except zucchini. I now know from firsthand experience that there is nothing to make you feel more triumphant and ferocious in the gardening world than growing an eleventy-ton squash. I swaggered around the patio and told the tomatoes to enjoy the ride this year, buckos, because next year it's nothing but squash all the way! That's right. Sayonara little piddly-ass plum tomatoes! Forget all about you, dumb won't-grow-for-nothing cucumbers. And okra, much as I love you, one pod does not a dinner make. Next year I am going to plant nothing but squash and watch the whole yard turn into a scary funhouse of funky, big zucchini.

And there is virtually no food on the planet that can't be made with zucchini. You can make spaghetti with zuke noodles instead of real pasta. You can make bread, cakes, muffins, puree, soup, stew—you name it, and you can probably put zucchini in it. But by far my favorite way to cook zucchini is to fry it. There's nothing finer than taking a fresh-from-the-garden wholesome nutritious vegetable and breading it and deep-frying it to golden perfection.

Deep-Fried Zucchini

THIS RECIPE WORKS BEST in a deep fryer, but I just cook them in a big frying pan with a pool of canola oil.

INGREDIENTS:

- All-purpose flour and spices (suggestions for spices: Tony Chachere all-seasoning, black pepper, cayenne pepper, or any spices you like)
- Yellow cornmeal (optional)
- Canola oil for frying
- 2 fresh medium-size zucchini squash cut into even-sized strips or chunks
- 2 eggs, beaten well in a shallow bowl

THE RECIPE:

Step 1: Combine all-purpose flour with generous amounts of your choice of spices to taste. You can also add in some yellow cornmeal to the mix. I have made this gluten-free with a mixture of corn flour, cornmeal, and rice flour, which only proves that when it comes to deep-frying, my love knows no bounds.

Step 2: Heat canola oil in a big frying pan over medium-high heat.

Step 3: Dip the cut zucchini into the beaten egg, dredge in the flour and spice mixture, and set aside on a plate until you have about half the squash battered.

Step 4: Test the oil by placing one battered piece in the pan. Oil should sizzle and bubble around it, but not splatter like crazy (if it splatters, it's too hot).

Step 5: Place as many pieces of zucchini in the pan that can swim together comfortably in the oil.

Step 6: Wait a long, patient amount of time for the zucchini to turn golden on one side. Don't turn until it's golden. *Do not do it*. Resist temptation. Don't turn the heat up either; it has to be a rolling boil, not a grease fire in the pan.

Step 7: When just golden, turn zucchini over.

Step 8: Wait patiently for the other side to brown lightly.

Step 9: Remove from the pan and drain on a plate layered with paper towels.

Eat your vegetables!

This Therapist Tolls for Thee

When I was about twenty-five, I worked in an office with a girl named Mary who was ten years older than me and about six inches taller. I'd never really had a conversation with her; we just saw each other in passing in the break room until one Tuesday when I found her in the ladies' room crying. She was locked in a stall sobbing. I kind of shuffled outside the door for a bit until finally I knocked on the stall and asked if she needed anything. I wasn't sure what to do. I was still fairly new to corporate life, and this wasn't covered in the Human Resources handbook.

"I'm sorry, I just need a minute," she sniffled. "My cat died."

I waited for her with Kleenex and offered to get her a coffee or water, and she finally came out of the stall and washed her face, and we didn't talk about it again, but I never forgot her. The world is divided into two groups for me: people who love animals and people who never understand what it's like to have a best friend covered in fur.

When my cat Roy died, it was like losing a member of my family. He had known me back when I could still wear pigtails without looking ridiculous. I loved that cat with his old-man snores and his big blue eyes. He could stand on his back legs and open door handles. He could purr so loud it would wake you up in the night. After he was gone, I didn't just cry in the bathroom stall at work; I cried nonstop. And you can't really tell people, "Hey! I'm having a nervous breakdown because my cat died!" without risking some serious ridicule. It's really something that only other pet people understand.

One night about a month after Roy died, I did that thing people do that they really, really regret the next day. I drank eight-tenths of a bottle of wine, and in a maudlin stupor, I drunk-dialed my friend Jennifer who has already listened to her life's work of drunk-dials from my Divorce Year, and then later I repeated the entire sorry mess with the one boyfriend from my past who I still speak to.

Each conversation went something like, "I was just watching this great movie on TV, and the main actress had all these friends, and they were so close, and she lived in that town her whole life, and Roy's gone, and I don't even go out for tacos anymore!"

Or something like that.

It was just that thing you do, that pathetic little drunken phone call in which you confess that you suspect you miss your cat more than you miss your ex-husband, your commute is sucking the lifeblood out of you, your ovaries are drying up and you don't even want children, and someone at work tried to tell you that you'll change your mind, and one day everything will be hunky-dory when you find Mr. Right and settle down, and so you spilled coffee on them "accidentally," because you were too weak-willed to just walk out and hijack an Oreo truck.

And that is when I decided that no one—not my parents, my friends, or my boyfriend from when I was eighteen and a size 6—should have to listen to me complain anymore, even if I was getting quite masterful at it. So I decided to see a therapist.

After all, this is Los Angeles. It is practically required that you see a therapist, date someone who is sexually deviant and/or was on a reality show, and go on the master cleanse at least once. (I once dated a guy who was on that old game show *Studs*. I thought he was joking, then he pulled out the VHS tape and made me watch the entire episode. Now I just have to go on the master cleanse, and I'll officially get my L.A. card.)

I called my insurance provider to get a list of therapists covered by my policy. I didn't mention that the impetus for this quest in self-realization was spawned by the loss of my cat. The insurance folks e-mailed me a PDF that was twenty-seven pages long. There was Marci in Sherman Oaks, Rolf in Van Nuys, and Carol in Studio City. And then there he was—Max Goldberg. That wasn't his real name, but it was very close. Listed beneath his hours was a notation that he also spoke Hebrew and Yiddish. I started to have warm, vaguely homey feelings of being comforted by Max, maybe over a nice bowl of chicken soup. Maybe his wife would invite me over for dinner and we'd all be blessed and happy, and I realize that what I am doing is picturing myself having dinner with Rabbi Shmuley in a scene from his TV show, *Shalom in the Home*. I love Rabbi Shmuley, and I'm pretty sure any man with eleventeen children must also love pets. I decide that the mention of Yiddish is a good sign, a harbinger of therapy success.

I called to make an appointment, and so far my therapy fantasy rabbi is coming true! He mentioned he was originally from Israel, and he had a thick Israeli accent, so comforting, so available on Saturdays! I immediately called my friend Jennifer, excited because I was certain I had found the Rabbi Shmuley of the Valley.

I was going to see Rabbi Therapist and be cured of my neuroses and set upon a path of goodness and less melancholia (which at sixty dollars an hour as a co-pay is not too much to expect).

I am fifteen minutes early for my first session with the rabbi. For the record, I do not know if he is a rabbi, but I keep envisioning him as a happy, centered, family-loving rabbi, father of eight, with a strong and loving marriage and a deep sense of the mystical, like the Kabbalah pre-Madonna. I think he will be wearing dark colors, have a beard, and be wearing a yarmulke. He will get me; he'll help me come up with socially acceptable things to tell people when I find myself crying about my cat. He'll understand that I'm not really lost, I just need to be pointed more clearly in the right direction, and that all this complaining is a mask for a greater lust for life, and so on.

I fidget. But not in a neurotic way.

Finally, I hear a door opening and out steps someone who closely resembles a Florida snowbird fresh from a game of shuffleboard down at the condo in Boca. He's wearing a bold flower-print shirt, khaki knee-length shorts, and white socks and tennis shoes.

"I'm Max. Are you Sheryl?" he asks.

"No, I'm Laurie."

"I thought I had Sheryl at 2:00 PM."

"Well, I'm not Sheryl, but I do have an appointment at 2:00 PM." Oh God. Is this the new Rorschach test for crazy? Make someone wait in the bland beige waiting room and then question their identity and the validity of their appointment?

But Max just shrugs and makes a joke about his failing memory (good start, all of it), and we spend the next ten minutes trying to get his copy machine to work so he can photocopy my insurance card.

It is a little underwhelming, this therapy stuff.

Finally, at 2:20 PM and exactly twenty-three dollars into our session, we sit down, and Dr. Goldberg begins to ask me detailed questions about why on earth a nice girl such as myself seems unhappy. It starts with the good doctor picking up a fresh yellow legal pad and a pen, and then he focuses on me for the first time, realizing at last that I am not Sheryl, I am not his secretary (yet I know how to use the copier), and I am here to see him about something.

"So, tell me why you're here."

And even though our session actually gets worse following what I am about to disclose to you, this next bit was likely the most humiliating thing I have done around a guy wearing a flowered shirt in a long, long time. I just started crying.

Crying. To Max from the shuffleboard squad in Boca.

I hate crying in front of people. I loathe crying. I do a surprisingly large amount of crying. I leak at the eyeballs during

moving Kodak commercials. I cry when I watch *Animal Planet*—
it doesn't even matter what's on! I cried during a particularly
heart-wrenching episode of *Pimp My Ride.*

I also cry when I'm mad. The worst mad crying happens at
work, and nothing says *I'm a Professional and Grown-up!* like crying in your boss's office. I have cried during my review, cried
because someone was mean and horrible to me in a meeting, and
cried because I was so mad I wanted to stash a coworker into the
shredder bin.

But the very worst crying is that awful moment you don't
expect to cry at all, for example, after you just helped your so-
called therapist work the magical load-letter drawer on his copy
machine. There's some strange mechanism in my tear ducts that
reacts with immediate fervor to a combination of simple, trained
focus and a gentle, "Is there anything wrong?"

So I cried. Officially producing a reason for attending therapy.

He pushed a box of Kleenex my way and asked me again, this
time with markedly more interest, "So. Tell me . . . what is the
matter here?"

And I gave him the brief history up to this point. I was a well-
trained Good Girl who spent a remarkable amount of my life
pleasing others, which led me to getting married and holding
down a very normal job and pretending to have a totally great life,
and I got married to a guy who was great on paper and then everything went wrong and there was the divorce, then I was crazy, then
I got better, then my cat died, then I had run out of traumatic
events and finally just said, "I have no idea what is wrong with me.
But I am going to be forty one day, and I have no idea what I am

supposed to do with my life or where I'm supposed to do it, and I'm tired of trying to please people because they're never satisfied, and sometimes I think about getting rid of all my clothes."

"But you're a pretty girl; you could still get married again, have kids."

Pardon me?

"Well, if you're still upset about this divorce, and you said you felt like you lost your identity, I think maybe you should think about meeting a nice boy; you still have time. How soon did you say you would be turning forty?"

And suddenly I wasn't crying anymore. I was just sitting, quietly, trying to decide if there was a hidden camera somewhere in the room and I was being filmed for one of those *Punk'd* rip-off shows on basic cable that put normal people in ridiculous situations and they are supposed to react with a morally accept-able response. In which case, I could not throw the Kleenex box at Dr. Max and lecture him on the rights of women, the sexual revolution (I was still kind of sketchy on that one myself), and this newfangled thing called You Don't Have to Be Married to Be a Viable Human Being.

So I just cleared my throat and shifted uncomfortably in my chair.

"I don't think the answer to all of life's unanswered questions is to get married and have babies. It seems like maybe we should have some other options. Don't you think? I mean, being married didn't make me happy, it just made me obsessively focused on someone else's happiness. Shouldn't it be acceptable for a woman to decide to be unmarried?"

"Do you take any drugs? Drink alcohol? Smoke?"

"Uh, let's see. I quit smoking more than a year ago. I don't take any drugs . . . well, I take Xanax when I fly . . ."

"Xanax? You have trouble with anxiety?"

"I have trouble with takeoff and landing, mostly, and the parts in between. It's just that I'd really prefer to interview the pilots first, you know, maybe give them a quick Breathalyzer, check underneath the airplane for large holes or ticking boxes, that sort of thing."

"I see."

Pause.

"Go on."

"Well, I take Motrin if I have a headache. Does that count?"

"Do you have headaches often?" This question-and-answer session seems really off-topic, but I answer anyway.

"Um, no. I don't think so. Sometimes red wine gives me a headache. I think it's the tannins. Or the red part. Which is probably the skin. But you need to get those antioxidants!"

"So you drink red wine? How often do you drink wine?"

"Oh, like in a lifetime?" I ask.

"Just a week. How much do you drink in, say, an average week?"

"Oh, I don't know. In a week I probably have about four glasses of wine," I answer. And he's staring at me with his glasses perched halfway down his nose. I can't tell if he's staring or trying to rack focus.

"And have you ever considered seeking help for this?" he says. "Or joining a twelve-step group?"

"Joining a twelve-step group for four glasses of wine a week? Doesn't that seem a little . . . expedited? I mean, if four glasses of wine in one week is what it takes to make you an alkie, then France is in serious trouble. And don't get me started on the Italians. They'd be looking at a good twenty-four steps."

Max laid down his yellow legal tablet and pen and looked at me. He had that practiced look of admonition mixed with kindly indulgence. He sort of looked like he was about to ask me to pass the salt and pepper. I don't think therapy is helping.

"Laurie, you see, doctors are trained to understand that when a patient estimates his or her consumption habits, it is usually half of the real amount. So we know to double or even triple the amount of drinking, eating, or recreational drug use a patient claims to have in a week's time frame or so. It's not uncommon for the patient to even believe they're really only consuming a small amount . . ."

"So you expect every person to lie to you?" I say.

"Well, not lie exactly, more like an underestimate . . ."

"But I thought therapy is where you pay someone to listen to you be honest for a change. Why would you lie in therapy?" This is so confusing!

"Oh! You wouldn't believe the stories . . ." he starts to say.

"No no, don't tell me the stories." I held up my hand, the official 1980s symbol for stop, in the name of love. "I'm not supposed to hear the stories. They're confidential. This is confidential right?"

"Yes," he says. Nodding. "Yes, of course."

"Okay, so let me revise my answer. I drink one glass of wine per week."

"Yes, but you already said you drink four glasses of wine."

"That was before I knew I had to lie."

And we finished what was to be both my first and last session with Dr. Max telling me that time was up, but that I should give some thought to why a perfectly healthy, normal girl with a good future who could even one day maybe snag a man again would need a therapist, instead of a husband.

Let's Get Physical

People in this town work out. They go to the gym and mention it in conversation, and other people don't look at them in awe and wonder; they just act like it is totally normal for human beings to drive to a place of mutual sweat and suspect hygiene, take off their clothes in a shared locker room with strangers, put on sweat-absorbing clothing and freakishly expensive shoes, and then sit on a bike and pedal to nowhere for twenty minutes.

The corporation I work at is located right in downtown Los Angeles, and we have a big, newly remodeled gym in the basement of our building. Lots of people from my office go there. Daily. And they see each other there, which freaks me out to no end. I can't imagine sweating in my sports bra and T-shirt while my boss or the mailroom guy or anyone I know is in the same room. Something about it seems too intimate and personal; *this person has seen me sweat. And now we are discussing a spreadsheet.*

And I sweat. Women aren't supposed to drip with sweat like a pro basketball player trapped in a sauna, but that's me. I have never been a delicate Southern rose who glistens becomingly in a heat wave. I sweat when I am nervous, I sweat when I am hot, and I pour buckets when I am forced to exercise. I like to fool myself into thinking this keeps my body free of toxins or helps my skin stay clear or some such, but in reality I would swap places in a heartbeat with one of those glistening, sweatless girls. Oh to be able to wear a silk blouse on a summer's day without the underarm shadow of despair and perspiration!

One day I walked into the little kitchen area in my office to get a mug of coffee, and two of my female coworkers were right in the middle of a conversation about the gym. They are both incredibly fit and do things like run and lift weights. They both go to the gym in our building and go to classes and see other coworkers there.

"I like the treadmill, but I just can't seem to break into a sweat on the treadmill," says Brunette Skinny Coworker.

I fill up my mug with coffee and watch like it's a show on TV; that is how unreal it seems to me. This is not my world.

"I know! I really have to hit the elliptical to get a good sweat, but I actually prefer the treadmill," says Auburn Skinny Coworker.

"I myself am breaking into a sweat just listening to ya'll talk," says Blonde Lazy Me. They laugh and then resume talking about the gym, and I resume sitting in my office chair and working on my secretary's spread.

As I sit in my office drinking coffee and thinking about my cute, thin, go-getter coworkers who work out and enthusiastically hope to find activities that make them sweat, I wonder if maybe I am missing out on something. People go to the gym and seem to like it. Maybe I could become someone who talks about the gym. I could even actually attend the gym. There's certainly no reason why at my age and state of entrenched couch-potato-ness, I can't turn over a new leaf and join a gym like everyone else and become aerobicized! thin! fit! toned! and perfect, like that old 1980s movie *Perfect* with John Travolta and Jamie Lee Curtis, which was probably the last time I ever seriously considered joining a gym. And I might feel endorphins, which will charge through my body in a rush of runner's high (because eventually I will be so fit and trim from all my time at the gym that I will do some running . . . well, once I find a bra that keeps me from giving myself a black eye when running), and maybe this is what I need. Maybe I really *need* the gym. Maybe this could change my life, like those inspiring stories in *People* magazine about normal folks who join a gym and one hundred pounds later, they're in skinny jeans and holding up a pair of old pants twice their size.

My office is beige and dark beige. Usually it closes in on me, makes me wonder if I am developing a pallor from the fluorescent lighting. But today I'm jittery in my chair. Maybe it's the coffee, maybe it's all this stuff about the gym. I've been trying new things to change my life but none of them have really involved lace-up shoes. Perhaps meditation is for people who are farther along the path of enlightenment. For those of us still looking for the off-ramp to the path to enlightenment, physical exertion and purity of exercise might be the answer!

This is what I am telling myself, anyway, as I hand over my debit card later that night and sign up for a one-month trial membership at a gym downtown four blocks from my office. I am not crazy enough to think I could get over my squeamishness at seeing coworkers in nonwork settings, so I have not even considered signing up at the gym in my building. In fact, as I stand there in the Hot Bodies Gym (not its real name), I am wondering if the coffee was spiked. Maybe I am making a grave error in judgment.

I try to get the guy behind the desk to let me sign up under a pseudonym.

"You want to pay for a membership for someone else?" he asks, perplexed.

"No," I said. "I want to pay for the gym membership for me, but I just want my own membership to be in a different name. Like Jane Doe—or, more appropriate—Dough, ha ha."

"Uh, I don't think we can do that. I have to ask my manager," he says.

"Can't you just take my money and then put a different name on my membership card?" I ask. This seems easy. This doesn't seem like something we need managerial input on.

"Why do you want a different name on the card if the membership is for you?" he asks.

"Just in case I am really bad at this," I tell him. "Then no one will remember it's me, they'll just remember Jane Dough."

"No one is bad at the gym, lady," he says, "You'll see, it's really easy."

And that is how I find myself several days later, using my own real name, standing on an elliptical machine and punching the ON button while nothing at all happens.

Finally, a red-shirted gym employee takes pity on me and comes over to help me turn on the machine.

"I'm pushing the ON button," I say defensively. I am already bad at the gym. Before long I'll start having hallucinations and flashbacks to seventh-grade gym class where all the kids wore the same horrible poly-blend zip-up gym suit and I tried to convince the volleyball coach I had cholera and needed to sit out. I am already sweating and I haven't even worked out yet!

The gym employee starts pressing buttons and suddenly the front of the machine lights up like an airplane about to take flight.

"Okay," he says. "Now just enter your weight and press the green button."

"Enter my weight? Like in pounds?" I can feel a small line of perspiration beginning to form right at my temples.

"Yeah, just use the keypad and punch it in." He is talking to me patiently, but his eyes are on the TV monitors mounted on the wall above the elliptical machines. They're all playing local news without the sound.

"Why on God's green earth would I tell the machine how much I weigh?" I am becoming shrill. I can hear the shrillness.

The red-shirted gym guy peels his eyes away from the basketball scores and looks at me. He talks to me like one would speak to a small, daft child.

"The machine calculates how many calories you burn when you work out based on your weight," he says.

"What is this? The *Scared Straight* of cardio? Are there other machines I can use that don't need to weigh me first?"

It is seven o'clock in the morning, and I am not telling anyone or anything how much I weigh today. I am on the verge of quitting the gym, and I have yet to actually use a single machine. I am, however, noticing an increased heart rate—and I am full-on sweating.

The patient red-shirted gym guy tries to explain to me in detail how it's best to just enter the information and then the machine will take my heart rate and on and on and on and I shake my head and say, "Okay, I weigh ninety pounds."

And he laughs. He doesn't mean to, but he laughs. Because I weigh ninety pounds in the left leg, at least.

"Fine, one hundred pounds even," I say. "That's it, that's my best offer."

He gives up. He leads me over to the treadmill where I can just push the ON button and it will start moving. And I walk on the treadmill for twenty minutes, which, according to the signs posted on every vertical surface, is the maximum allotted time for cardio equipment, and I wonder why I have just paid for a monthlong gym membership when all I have done so far is walk for twenty minutes on a treadmill that is identical to the one sitting in my living room and currently holding up my black jacket and two scarves.

There are many things I admire about the gym, though. I like the neat spray bottles and paper towels they have mounted around the facility. Ideally, these are to be used for cleaning off the equipment after you use it, but I wait all week for someone to approach the little nook of disinfectant and no one does. Maybe they use it more during the afternoon when it's warmer outside and presumably people sweat more. This is what I tell myself.

My favorite part of the gym is telling people you went there. I've been trying to work it into everyday conversation, but I'm still new to this. By Thursday my opportunity finally arises. A woman standing at the bus stop is staring at her wristwatch impatiently. She turns and asks me what time it is, because the bus is a little late. I tell her it's 6:17 AM.

"Is the bus late?" she asks.

"Yes," I tell her. "I was hoping to be at the gym right about now."

She turns and goes back to staring at her watch. By the time the bus arrives and then drives us all downtown, I make it to the gym to discover I have just enough time to walk on the treadmill for five minutes before showering, and I have to shower because I've lugged ten pounds of toiletries and a work outfit with me on the cross-town bus. It's sort of a moral imperative to justify being a slave to my own vanity.

The next day, I change up my schedule and arrive at the gym at 6:30 AM. To get there at 6:30 AM, I had to wake up at 4:45 AM, stare at the clock for seven long minutes before even being able to roll out of bed, and drive into work a full hour and a half early. The cats glance at me and fall back asleep as I pack my gigantic nylon bag and bring a smaller version of my home bathroom to the gym with me. Shampoo, conditioner, soap, moisturizer, travel hair dryer, flip-flops, towel, plastic bags for holding towels after use, smaller towel for gym sweat, wet wipes to disinfect machines before touching. An outfit for work on top, where it will hopefully have less time to wrinkle.

By the time I get to the gym and stuff my gigantic bag of personal items into the locker, I am exhausted and craving those little hash browns from McDonald's and some cheese. I don't know how people do this every day. I need about two more hours of sleep.

The locker room has a long, blue hallway that delivers you right into the middle of the gym. I walk into the aerobic machine area and scan the room for empty pockets. I don't like to stand right next to someone if it's avoidable. It's like the spacer stall—if the whole row of bathroom stalls is empty except one, why would you choose the stall right next to the lone occupied stall? Put a spacer stall between you. I think the spacer stall is just good manners.

In one corner of the room I watch a woman work vigorously on an elliptical machine. She's energetic, and her clothes are coordinated and cute. I think maybe I should try the elliptical again. I recall my two colleagues saying they got a great workout on it. Perhaps we have different fitness goals, but I am here, and I might as well try it. They were both really fit, both exercise people. My primary objectives with this whole gym situation are to remain healthy enough to get into my pantyhose without getting winded and to try something new. I'm not interested in comparing muscles or sporting a six-pack, I just want to remain physically fit enough so that my thighs don't rub together and hinder me when I'm running toward that big twice-yearly sale at Bloomies.

There is an elliptical in the back row of machines with a cushion of two empties on each side. I get up on the contraption and push the buttons like I saw Red Shirt do a few days ago. I enter a completely fictional weight (I think I weighed that amount when I was nine years old) and push the buttons in sequence as they light up, and before long I start pedaling-walking. It's my first time on an elliptical machine, and it's a little like riding a bike while standing upright, all on a trampoline. I keep up with the machine for a while, although it takes rather more coordination than I would have expected. I am beginning to get a little breathless, though I can't tell how much is my actual effort and how much is centrifugal force, which starts to interest me, because this isn't a natural movement for me, and I feel like I'm being pulled along to keep up. So as a test I decide to stop pedaling all at once, and I kind of stiffen my legs. This is not a good idea. I discover it a little too late, because the machine is still in motion, and I trip forward a bit with the pull, then overcorrect to stay upright, and all of a sudden I am ass-down on the floor mat.

I look up and see a gym patron and two employees hurrying my way. The red-shirted guy from a few days ago is one of the people who are rushing to my aid. It's all happening so fast. My first thought is not, *Am I okay? Have I broken anything?* All that goes through my mind is, *I just fell off the easiest machine in the gym and I can never, ever return here again.* And the machine is still going. I can see my water bottle sitting there in the cup holder and my towel draped over the control panel, and I am looking up at all this from my vantage point on the floor.

Three people help me up. They ask if I am okay. I nod and try to die of embarrassment but instead I live, and I go to the locker room and put on my flip-flops and attempt to take a shower without anyone seeing me naked. I thought falling off gym machines was an urban myth! I wonder if I can get my money back for the month. I wonder if I have actually broken anything besides my pride. I wonder if the elliptical machine is still going, still thinking an imaginary 106-pound woman is working out like a champ.

Obviously unable to return to the downtown gym, I discover my little elliptical incident has turned into a lucky change of events. The gym I signed up with is a chain. They have locations all over Los Angeles and most of them seem to be in the most ghetto corner of every zip code. One is remarkably close to where I live.

After dragging my giant duffel bag to and from the office every day for a week, I am happy to try the gym closest to my house and see if that works better. I figure I can leave home in my workout clothes, go to the gym, and then come back and shower in peace in my own bathroom with all my own stuff and no protective flip-flops. That way I can go to work without all the luggage. And of course there is the small matter of being able to start all over again fresh and new. I decide to ignore the fact that I am already having to switch gyms barely a week into my membership. Instead, I am hoping this change will make me more excited about the money I forked over in a caffeine-induced fit of insanity.

The first morning at my ghetto hometown gym, I have a most pleasant surprise: a guy who looked exactly like a short, thin Asian Antonio Banderas got on the treadmill right in front of me (so I had the perfect view). He could have stayed there for six hours and I would have remained there, walking like a dedicated mouse around and around, just for the view. It was and may be the only time I logged an hour on the treadmill. He was yummy. And no one in this gym seems to heed the twenty-minute machine limits, so I just wait until the good-looking guy tires out and I quit walking.

The best part about the gym is clear within the first visit. It offers me the most unusual people-watching opportunities. There is a visual cornucopia of madness at the ghetto gym. I wish I could take my digital camera in and sneak pictures of folks so I'd have a visual aid when talking to my friends or my parents. Most of all I love to watch what people wear at the gym. I am incredibly boring and mousy with my workout gear—black track pants, gray or black T-shirt, sometimes a gray sweatshirt. I am the soulless Muzak of the treadmill world. But my ghetto home-town gym is filled with fashion extroverts in tight, body-hugging Lycra. There is a woman who wears pantyhose and a pastel bodysuit every day, and the pantyhose have the built-in panty control top, so you see the reinforced part sticking out four inches below her bodysuit. I am fascinated by this. I wonder if she only has one of those mirrors that show the top half. Or maybe she likes the look. It's impossible to know for sure without asking her about it, and I don't see myself crossing that boundary line anytime soon. On the few days I don't see her at the gym, I wonder if she was there earlier in a different-colored leotard with her reinforced pantyhose on. The idea of working out in pantyhose makes me itch.

There are a lot of sexy ladies at the gym, even that early in the morning. Some arrive wearing more makeup than I wear to work. I saw one woman in her late fifties or early sixties and she was in great shape, the shape I am trying to be in. She was wearing black shiny tights with a tight T-shirt and a leather belt looped around her waist. She was working it, and it worked for her. Later I saw her making out with a guy in the corner of the weight room, which made me wonder if she was actually *working it*, like for an hourly rate. One can never be sure.

My neighborhood gym is crowded, somewhat scary, and slightly intimidating, but it is never dull. I assumed that since this is Los Angeles, and particularly the San Fernando Valley, most of the folks at this gym would be actors and actor-hopefuls, walking on the treadmill at a slow enough pace to either talk about their latest audition with another struggling actor while appearing to work out but not actually sweat (thereby becoming gross and sticky), or maybe they would be Hollywood hopefuls scanning the room for people they know or want to know.

The day before I ventured to my neighborhood gym, I pictured good-looking twentysomethings reading a script casually on the StairMaster, which has the optimal surface for propping up the script so everyone can see that they are Very Important and Read Scripts.

My gym surprised me with a completely different crowd.

The location was the first tip-off. My new gym is strategically located in a shopping center that experienced not one but two fatal shoot-outs in the span of two weeks' time. It is right next door to a grocery store that was recently covered in broken glass and yellow crime-scene tape.

I haven't told my parents this news. They may think I'm crazy to go to this gym. But I think it is serendipity. What are the chances of another fatal shoot-out happening in that exact same location again anytime soon? I look at it as a good thing—my gym has already been pre-crimed. I believe we got all the fatal shootings out of the way and now the odds are in my favor. It is probably the safest gym in the area.

And there are no hipster see-and-be-seen actors at my new gym. Instead, the entire gym is filled with people *actually* working out. People who are in shape. Male people. Very buff, very attractive, somewhat scary, somewhat menacing males with tattoos lifting weights everywhere.

These guys are serious about working out.

I went to the gym downtown for almost a whole week and never once saw anyone lift free weights. My neighborhood version of the gym has an entire floor devoted to the grunting, preening, and strutting guys who heft big round pieces of metal. It's sort of primal and foreign, watching them watch themselves in the mirrors, perfecting their weight-lifting form as their arms or legs bulge with the Power. I am beginning to understand why people come to the gym on a regular basis without complaining about it at every possible opportunity, as I had been doing. Until now. I almost have a desire to lift a weight. As I walk on the treadmill, I pretend to read my creased copy of the *Economist* while I sneak glances at the guys pumping iron. I wonder if I could learn the lingo, be someone's spotter (the only word I know that in any way correlates with weight lifting). Maybe I would grow muscles, develop strength, or at least be able to defend myself in the parking lot.

Then I watch a sweaty guy who is twice my size use his perspiration-drenched towel to "wipe down" the bench he's just been dripping on. He swirls the sweat around and moves on to his next target. I decide there isn't enough Clorox in the world. But I still watch them.

The most disconcerting aspect of my newfound gym-rat life (can one be termed a gym rat after nine consecutive days on a treadmill and one day falling off an elliptical?) is the locker room. Have you ever thought to yourself, *Here I am in public with lots of strange women around me in workout clothes; now would be an excellent time to walk around naked and try to have random conversations about the weather.*

That has never crossed my mind. Now, however, I spend most of my time trying to avoid the locker room. I make sure I go to the bathroom before I leave my house, I try not to drink too much water while I'm there so I can hold it until I get home, and I have stopped bringing a purse that I have to lock up in the dreaded locker room. I now bring a tiny little canvas bag with a handle that hangs over the side of the treadmill, and I keep my keys and ID in there. It seems I found the gym where almost every female walks into the locker room and immediately becomes an aggressive nudist. I try not to judge, really I do, but I am simply not from a naked family. I wasn't even allowed to wear crop tops in high school because they were too revealing . . . and I thought that was reasonable.

I only survived the locker room for two days, and then I came up with my nakedness avoidance strategy. I think it was the group of women comparing stretch marks while one of them brushed her teeth—all the while buck-naked as the day they were born. Only much older. The few clothing-preferred folks like myself were trying to look at the floor and not touch anything. I still have not recovered from the shock.

Like all good things—and bad things—my monthlong trial at the Hot Bodies Gym finally came to an end. I paid for the full month and made it to the gym nineteen times successfully, one time for just five minutes and one time in which I fell off the elliptical. I felt like I got my money's worth; that is how I think—always the dutiful, penny-pinching frugalist getting her money's worth. I was secretly relieved when the last day of the thirty-day trial period came and went and I could sleep in for two extra hours in the morning and stop worrying about having to make an unplanned potty break and accidentally seeing thirty different versions of naked-stranger lady parts.

If all my time pretending to read the *Economist* while on the treadmill had taught me anything, it was that it is silly to pay for something that makes you feel inadequate, embarrassed, and inept in front of many strangers in spandex (and out of it) when you can have the same experience for free at home, without ever encountering other people and their sweat. I have a treadmill at home, and it is already paid for, and I can use that without having to disinfect it each time. I don't use it, but that isn't the point. The point is that if I did walk on it, and if I did fall off it, nobody would care. And I can use the bathroom anytime I need to. This is a good lesson to learn.

It was an excellent social experiment, though. In the end, I was happy I had spent the money to explore gym life. I got to mention to a few coworkers that I work out, which was fun until they asked me why they'd never seen me at the gym in our building and I had to make up something real quicklike to explain why I chose the Other Gym Company. I got to watch large men in damp T-shirts lift weights in front of mirrors. I felt like I experienced a whole other side of life, one in which people cheerfully stand on machines and spin, or ellip, or walk to nowhere with determined enthusiasm. I no longer could turn up my nose at gyms without ever having actually smelled one.

I have smelled it, I have seen it, I have determined I am not of it. I just wish the Hard Bodies Gym would get the memo. Every other day they send me letters or call and want to know why, *why* haven't I renewed my membership for the low, low rate of $69.99? They're more persistent than bill collectors.

My only regret about my time at the gym is that I didn't insist on a pseudonym and a fake mailing address—as it turns out, my instincts were right all along.

Class and No Class

My gym membership had the unexpected benefit of making me feel like a person who goes places to do physical activities. It's not true in the strictest sense, but I like the idea of being someone who goes to exercise-type classes. I especially love the idea of taking salsa classes with some dark, handsome stranger who may or may not have been part of an undercover operation to expose a drug cartel and now he's dancing for his life. Mostly, I watch TV and make up stories in my head about me wearing strappy high heels and twirling like one of those pretty half-naked girls on *Dancing with the Stars*.

Los Angeles is dotted from end to end with sports and fitness places that offer classes in everything from stripper aerobics to boxing. I get fliers in the mail about local places, and the Valpak coupon envelope is always good for at least one Pilates ad sandwiched between colorful brochures for lap-band surgery and teeth whitening.

The most promising flier didn't arrive in the mail; it was one I picked up at the pet food store near my house. The cover showed a cute terrier puppy lying on a yoga mat with a tan, smiling blond. The front of the brochure advertised doggy-and-me yoga classes, and I wondered if this was a new Southern California craze or if canine owners across the country were taking Downward Dog to a new place. I picked up the flier, planning to send it to my newly dog-crazed parents.

My folks always tolerated our childhood menagerie of pets, but they never actively yearned for a new dog or cat of their own; instead one would just show up occasionally, often following me home, since I was born with an internal magnet for all strays, both animal and human. Over the years we've had sea monkeys and baby turtles, and once a Fire Belly Newt who escaped and was discovered months later, petrified like a dusty relic under the laundry-room sink.

My little brother was the last one in the parental nest for ten years, and his dog passed away just before he left for college. The realization of everyone leaving, even the dog, might have been sad and depressing for some parents. Not mine. You could almost see the empty-nest euphoria beginning to take over, transforming my sensible, steady parents into wild and crazy born-again teenagers. It's not that they didn't love us, but there had been a whole lot of years devoted to our care and upkeep—and we had been *expensive*. When my youngest brother graduated from college, my parents bought a motor home and started driving around the country like people just set free from prison. A nice, loving prison of their own making, but still. Free at last!

They surprised us all when they decided just a year into their jailbreak to adopt a little Welsh corgie puppy. They named him Chivas, like their brand of scotch, and in mere days he had become the favored child, my brothers and I taking a distant and lonely second place to a furry mass of ears and teeth on top of the shortest, cutest legs you have ever seen on a living animal.

The dog has even brought my parents and me closer, because now they understand why I pay a British ex-pat in Woodland Hills thirty-five bucks a day to visit my cats when I am on vacation or away for even a weekend. I confided to my mom that my cat sitter's accent makes me think of charming British nannies from old Disney movies, and it feels more reassuring than leaving the cats in the care of a teenager named Marci who hopes to get on *American Idol* next season. My mom tells me on the phone that she and Dad don't leave the dog alone in the motor home for more than an hour because he gets lonely, and she's afraid he'll retaliate by chewing her sandals or eating his own poop. My parents and I have reached a crazy, happy place of mutual understanding brought on by our shared love of the Furminator.

So I had planned to send my folks the funny dog-yoga brochure, but when I got home I started flipping through it and noticed the little yoga studio's list of classes, most of them completely canine-free, one of which was offered just for beginners every Saturday morning for less money than I pay my cat sitter per day. Yoga is one of the few exercise-related activities I truly enjoy. You don't have to do any running or jumping and it's not a team sport, so if you're the weak link in the Warrior Pose, nobody cares. I took my first yoga class back in college, and we all used beach towels instead of mats and I felt really great afterward, like I had just expanded my horizons and become cutting-edge, and I didn't fall, pull a muscle, or embarrass myself in class. That is really my main criteria for successful activities.

For the first few years after I moved to L.A., I tried to take a yoga class every few months, but eventually I stopped. Years had passed since I'd last stretched out flat on a yoga mat or stood quietly to salute the sun. There had been a time in the months before my divorce when I went to yoga almost every single week, sometimes twice a week. I had even signed up for a whole series of classes at an upscale yoga studio on Ventura Boulevard. As I flipped through the brochure with the smiling terrier and smiling blonde on the cover, I couldn't remember exactly why I quit going. Maybe it was the commute, or the divorce, or just the daily grind. I didn't even own a yoga mat anymore.

The next best thing to actually being fit is preshopping in preparation of becoming fit. I decided to try a dogless beginner's yoga class, and to lay the groundwork, I went to Target and roamed around the fitness supplies aisles, comparing yoga mats and Pilates mats (I bought a Pilates mat because the foam was thicker). I also bought a pale blue cotton yoga mat holder with a vaguely Indianish symbol embroidered on a panel on the front. I decided against the Buddha T-shirt and the foam blocks, because I had no idea what they were used for.

Just the very idea of attending a yoga class again made me feel good. It's like combining meditation and the gym into one convenient package. And it's a known quantity, something I have done before, not like that awful Spinning class I took while I was exploring the options on my thirty-day gym membership. Spinning class sounded good—I can actually ride a bicycle, even more so if it remains stationary—but I didn't realize that spinning was so *aggressive*. And loud. The room at my neighborhood gym is small, and they close the door and turn the lights out and it heats up like a sweatbox. People get on the bikes and lean forward, butts off the seat. I didn't know that part, either. I thought the entire point of the bike was that it had a seat and one should use it for sitting. What is the purpose of standing up on a bike?

The music starts to play and it's loud and a hyperkinetic skinny person in spandex mounts a stationary bike in the front of the room—standing on the pedals, never sitting on the seat— and yells at everyone in the class for forty minutes. This particular Spinning instructor wore one of those little cordless microphones that attach to your head like Julie, the Time-Life operator. I thought I might have a panic attack after the first five minutes, but I was too scared to leave and be singled out for my unworthiness. The people in the class were just as excited and fired up as the instructor; they were all shouting in unison with her and pedaling furiously as they moved their bodies up and down and never once rested on the seat. I burned more calories from sheer fright than any real effort on my part. One of the few good things about being chunky and uncoordinated at the gym is that no one really expects you to be great at anything, so no one singles you out for sitting and resting. But I knew I couldn't leave. When the forty minutes was over I almost cried with gratitude.

Yoga is much more my speed. I like the whole thought of it, the pace and the slow poses held while each person concentrates on breathing. And people of every shape and size take yoga classes. There are plenty of trim, lithe girls in skintight organic cotton workout pants, but there are also old people and chubby people and folks like me who get out of breath from the sitting poses.

Before my first beginner's yoga class, I unwrapped my new mat from the plastic shrink-wrap and unspooled it onto the living room floor. I tried to lay on it and scoot around a bit to take the newness off it. Some cat hair stuck to the bottom and it looked a little less fresh, so I curled it into its fancy mat holder and dressed for class. I wore the same stuff I used for the gym, but with a tank top under my T-shirt so that just in case my T-shirt decided to ride up on some forgotten pose, I wouldn't be exposing the whole class to my marshmallow middle. I like being prepared. Pre-paration is the socially acceptable cousin of procrastination, but they both come from the same place. The need to feel in control and the desire to avoid are just opposite sides of the same coin. One really messed-up coin with a deep fear of failure.

Beginner's yoga was uneventful, which is a success. Three other women in the class brought the same multicolored mat I used. The poses were a little harder to maintain because I was doughier than the last time I'd attended yoga, but I was still smoking back then and skinnier. Smoking had made the breathing part of yoga a little harder, but my thighs were smaller and fit better under my also-smaller butt. Aside from that, beginner's yoga was a winner. On the way out I paid for a book of classes—five to start with—and promised myself I'd attend all five classes and not let the tickets expire after spending two years in the back of my junk drawer. Unlike the gym, yoga didn't require me to wake before the sun, and it didn't have a locker room situation or a scary parking lot. And I could leave the class and still go to the grocery store on the way home without worrying about being drenched in sweat.

The best part about yoga was the peaceful, relaxed feeling afterward. Back when I used to take yoga classes regularly, I would go home after classes and sit outside and smoke, which in retrospect seems self-defeating, but I still miss it. They're both peaceful, calming activities, but only one of them makes people look at you with naked disgust. After class, I think about how long it will be until I turn sixty-five and can smoke again, and I feel only a little shame. Not much, though.

The following Wednesday I left work a little early and made it just in time for the evening beginner's class. Midway through the mat poses, we were all lying prone on the mats and curving up with our backs as we brought one knee forward. And right then someone in the class released the loudest, most melodic fart I had ever heard. The entire class froze in suspended silence. Suddenly I remembered exactly why I had stopped going to the fancy yoga studio on Ventura Boulevard. Not because I farted, which would have made a fine, if embarrassing story, but because I *laughed* at someone who farted. I laughed the loud, spontaneous way you do without first wondering if it is appropriate to be laughing. And as soon as I realized that no, it was really *not* okay to these people (who take yoga very seriously) that I was laughing at a perfectly natural bodily function, I tried to stop laughing, but I couldn't. I was too far gone. I had become that horrible girl who keeps on trying to be quiet in a serious situation but ends up laughing so hard she's crying, tears streaming down her cheeks and sides hurting from laughing so hard. I was that awful, disrespectful girl.

I was asked to leave the fancy yoga studio. And I was at least recognizant of enough of my upbringing to know I had crossed a line and I could never, ever return to that place again. But I was still laughing. I laughed in my car, the whole way home. Then I had a cigarette because I really was that terrible girl.

So when the fart escaped in the middle of my new beginner's yoga class, I remembered I had four unused class tickets left in my wallet, totaling more than eighty dollars already spent—nonrefundable. If I started laughing, I told myself sternly, I would lose eighty dollars. And if I wanted to take yoga, I would have to once again look for a new place to go, and by now I was getting tired of having to change locations every time I tried some new form of exercise. I looked down and stared at my yoga mat, trying not to laugh, trying to remember how much I paid for the mat and its fancy faux-hippie holder and added that to my unclaimed eighty dollars of class tickets.

And then the miraculous happened. The teacher of beginner's yoga laughed. The *teacher* laughed!

"It happens," she said cheerfully. A few people giggled, and I realized I was not going to get kicked out if I giggled a little, too. *Farts are funny. I am not alone. I will not lose eighty dollars.* It was almost enough to stop holding my breath while the fear of fart smell passed.

"Now wrap your right arm through the space beneath your left knee and turn slowly to the left . . ." said the instructor. And class continued on. Eventually I had to breathe again, and I did, and the fart passed into history. *I love yoga,* I thought to myself.

Of all the machines and classes and sweat-inducing activities I have paid for, yoga is by far my favorite. I feel good after yoga. I feel capable. I don't fear I'll fall off something or have to tell anyone my true weight, and I bring my own mat so it's hygienically more appealing. I even found a yoga class at a community college nearby that does the entire session in the dark! It's not really dark in the room; the big gymnasium is surrounded by windows, but the class takes place at dusk and the instructor keeps the overhead fluorescent lights off. You spend the hour focused on the sound of her voice, and you can't see too well so there's not a lot of time spent comparing your Warrior Pose to anyone else's.

Of all my resolutions, yoga and zucchini have so far been the year's biggest winners.

The Things We Do

My greatest fantasy in life is lying on a beach in Mexico while a tan waiter wearing only red bikini pants brings me drinks with umbrellas in them, and the drinks are all in pineapples or coconuts.

Some people dream of world peace or ending hunger and some people dream of living in a chateau in the French countryside. I dream of all those things, too, of course, but above all, always, is the man in red bikini pants.

I have decided not to spend another Christmas at Grandma's house. Instead, I am going on a holiday vacation, alone, to a beach. Not a beach in Mexico, but a beach in Hawaii. And I am going alone, my second cheapskate vacation all by myself in a year.

Before my trip to Hawaii, I try on my bathing suit at home and look in the mirror. Even with the lights dimmed and the mirror tipped at a flattering angle, I can see the main problems.

The first one is my blinding neon whiteness. I have parts that haven't been exposed to the sun in years. I suspect that if I were to turn out all the lights and stand here in my bathing suit, I may glow in the dark. The other issue is the crop of unseemly hairs that escape the spandex encasement of the bathing suit. Specifically in the bikini line area. Not that this floral one-piece is cut as high as a bikini, but still, there is grooming to attend to.

Sometimes I fear that I will get busy on a project or some new endeavor and focus so intently on it that I'll forget the constant upkeep required for females to look smooth and less apelike, and I'll wake up one day with dreadlocks on my leg hairs and have eyebrows that have furrowed together like Bert from *Sesame Street*.

So before vacation, there is still more work to be done. I start by casually asking my friends if they've ever used self-tanner. One of my girlfriends tells me a long story that ends with, "and my hands stayed orange for four weeks!" I know my limitations as a person, and I don't overestimate my expertise in the color arena. I once spent an entire summer in junior high with orange hair—not red, or reddish, or goldenrod, but real orange hair—after a home hair-color experiment went awry. And I learned then that orange is not a good color for me.

After a little searching, I find a place close to my home that offers the spray tan done by a machine. I call to double-check that it's not self-tanner applied by another person, because the idea of some stranger rubbing me down with fake tan is too painful to imagine. They confirm that it's a machine, and I make an appointment for two days before I get on the plane.

Then I make an appointment for a bikini wax. I don't even have to ask my friends where to go for that, because I spent the entire year during my divorce sitting on my back patio and smoking cigarettes while reading stack after stack of glossy tabloid magazines. If I learned anything from that period in my life, it was the name and location of *the* salon where all the celebs go to get waxed: Pink Cheeks. I remembered it because it's in the Valley, and it's just a few doors down from one of my favorite art shops. The girl who answers the phone when I call to make an appointment is cheerful and informs me they only have one opening in the time slot I need, and that's the day before my trip. As a precaution I go online and order a little brown sarong for my bathing suit. I have been down the rocky road of hair removal before, and if all else fails, I will at least be able to hide the evidence.

The day of my spray tan appointment, I am late for work because I spend twenty minutes vigorously exfoliating my entire body with a loofah. According to all my research online, the spray stuff can get blotchy if you have patchy skin, and I don't want to scare Hawaiians and tourists alike with blotches. The horror.

After work, I drive to the tanning salon. When I get there I am given complete instructions on how to use the machine by a girl who looks like she is fourteen. She's perfectly tan with little white teeth, and she is wearing Playboy bunny earrings. She carefully explains how to apply the blocking lotion to my hands and feet so I won't end up with telltale tan hands. There's a shower cap for my hair, and towels hanging neatly from a rack.

She explains how to push the button and how to stand for the most even application.

"Try not to breathe while you're in there, too" she says. "You don't want to inhale all that stuff."

Then she asks me what level I want.

"Level?"

"It's what level of tan we use for you," she explains.

"Oh. Well, what do you recommend?" I am asking a child with Playboy earrings for her tanning advice.

"Um, you're pretty light," she says, shaking her head. "I'd start with level one; you don't want to overdo it."

I concur with her and she leaves and I lock the door and begin to undress. Everything is very clean and tidy in the room, which is reassuring. I put my hair up in the shower cap, careful not to cover my face. The blocking lotion is a little trickier, because I don't want orange palms but I don't want completely tan arms that end in dramatic white hands. I work the lotion around my toes and feet as instructed, then I get into the machine.

It's a tall metal box with nozzles on the inner walls and a few lighted buttons. I slide the door shut and try to stand like I saw the tan girl demonstrate. I can smell the chemicals in there, and I start to feel a little edge of panic, because I am in a smallish metal box alone with some self-tanner spray. I imagine this is what it feels like to be a glazed ham. I push the buttons and the spray begins. I try not to breathe it in, though I do a little. The whole process lasts about a minute or less and then it's over and the box clears out and you're done. I washed off the lotion from my hands and feet and then used the towels to dry off. Back in my clothes I feel a little sticky and I smell like self-tanner, but I am still a ghostly shade of white.

The next morning is a completely different story. I am . . . *golden*. Luscious golden tan with just a few minor blotches around my left ankle. I am shocked and happily amazed at the results. Spray tan must contain a little crack, too, because after just one hit I'm hooked. I admire my legs in the full-length mirror. They aren't any smaller but without all the blinding marshmallow skin they're less obvious. My spray tan is not dark and tropical, but it is just enough color to assure others I am not in fact made entirely of mayonnaise. I am pleased and happy and ready for vacation.

Now there is just the small matter of the bikini waxing. My appointment is in the afternoon, and I am comforted by the small fact that whoever has to see my lower half unclothed will at least be looking at a golden summer tan.

Pink Cheeks is a Valley legend, and after hearing so much about it, I am surprised to discover that the waiting room is tiny—barely room for four people to sit in awkward silence. I give the girl at the desk my name and then I stand in front of a display of candles and lotions and a rack of tongue scrapers for sale.

Finally I am called and the girl who meets me at the desk is friendly and cute in what looks like pastel-printed hospital scrubs.

"I'm Allison," she says. "Right this way!" and we walk down a narrow and discreetly decorated hallway and into a private, heated room.

"So what are you having today?" she asks.

"Um, a bikini wax," I say.

"Are you having a Brazilian? A Playboy? A pseudo?" she asks.

"I am not sure," I tell her. I am pretty sure I know what a Brazilian is, but isn't that the same as a Playboy?

"Is this your first time here?" she asks, and I nod and she hands me a little preprinted card with descriptions and names. "This is our menu."

"Oh, there's a menu," I say, relieved. Then, "Oh Lord, ya'll do everything . . ."

"We sure do!" she says. And I tell her I'm leaving for vacation tomorrow and I want to be able to wear a bathing suit without scaring the other tourists—from a hair management perspective, anyway.

"Okay, I'd suggest a pseudo," she says. "Just get undressed from the waist down and lay back on the table and I'll be right back."

I do as I am told, wondering as I do how many jobs in this city involve someone telling you to get undressed so you can somehow beautify some part of yourself. This is the second time in two days I have been instructed on how to get naked to look better for a vacation in which I don't plan to be naked at all. Maybe next year I will go on vacation to somewhere cold, like Prague or Helsinki, and all the advice I'll get in the days leading up to my trip will be about how to wear more clothes.

Allison returns and gets started. One day aliens will arrive from outer space to study human earthling behavior and one of the more remarkable aspects of their time here will be discerning why women voluntarily pay to visit a stranger who covers delicate portions of the body in hot wax and rips it off to remove hair.

The hot wax also removes most of my golden spray tan right in the bikini area.

"Whoops!" says Allison. "Looks like we're losing your tan!"

I prop up on one elbow and look down at the square white swathe of smooth, hairless skin that still stings from the wax.

"You have got to be kidding me."

"Well, you have some options here," she says seriously. I gather from her tone this is not the first time she has seen this problem before. "You can apply a small amount of self-tanner this evening right to the paler areas, or you can exfoliate to lighten the tanned skin."

"I was so golden and tanned!" I lean back on the table and sigh. The sarong arrived yesterday so at least I will be able to cover the color-blocked area. I briefly consider abandoning the rest of the bikini wax, but I don't want to be uneven. So we continue on.

Allison applies more hot wax and continues ripping the hair off my bikini line.

"It will even up some in the shower," she suggests.

In two more minutes she's done and she pats my leg. "All set!" she says. "Did you want to get your butt done?"

"Pardon me?"

"Your butt. You want that done too?"

"I don't think I have a very hairy butt," I say. "Is that a problem? Butt-cheek hair?"

"For some people. But what I mean is on the inside."

"You mean *up the butt?*" I am horrified. I think this is a joke. If there are hidden cameras and I am being pranked, I will die right here on this table from sheer embarrassment.

"You should try it," she reassures me. "It's very smooth and hygienic."

"You mean you wax the inside of people's butt cheeks? They pay you to do that?"

"Every day!" she says.

Twenty minutes later I am sitting in my car with the key in the ignition, hands on the wheel, still parked out back of the salon. I call my mother.

"You will not believe what just happened to me," I tell her. "I just paid sixty dollars to get a bikini wax and then you flip over on all fours and this person—a complete stranger—waxes your butt!"

"They wax your butt cheeks?" she asked. This is just not something I have ever heard of, and apparently neither has my mom.

"Oh no, they wax *up the butt*." I have never said these words to anyone before today and now I am saying them to my mom. "I mean this woman has just seen more of me than any other human on earth, including my ex-husband!"

"That is just wrong!" she says. "Why do people do that?"

"I'm not sure," I say. "I think I might be in shock."

"Well, I know I am," she says. "I'm not sure people need to be doing things like that. It seems unnatural. And painful."

And we chatted for a few minutes more, then I told her I had to go and buy some self-tanner at the drugstore and apply it to my hairless and now tanless bikini line.

And then, finally, I could pack and go on my vacation and stop worrying about my grooming and my tan and hairy butts and just drink fruity things out of pineapples and never speak of it again.

Vacation: Far, Far Away

I am in Maui . . . right now I hear the surf, the ocean, the wind . . . it's extraordinary. Dinner was a piece of baked fish, a scoop of rice, and something frothy from a coconut.

Earlier today I went to the beach—after all, I'm here; how can one come to Hawaii and not frolic in the sand? It seems like a visitor to this little island paradise would be handed a citation upon exiting the airport: "Improper exiting of properties and unadvantageous use of beach."

I put on my bathing suit, a chocolate brown tropical monstrosity purchased off the Internet, this time using as close to my real measurements as possible, and even still, the suit is almost too small—snug—but keeps everything in place. The bikini wax was so invasive I'm not sure I'll ever need to groom for a bathing suit again. The beach was quiet and fairly empty and no one pointed and stared at my uneven tan in the bikini-line area.

So today I woke up early, the sky was rainy and gloomy, and the wind was blowing so hard that the palm trees bent nearly in half. It was wild, untamed, as if the resorts and their carefully trained staffs of Hawaiian-shirted boys and girls were nothing in the face of weather. The weather: It's the real dictator of the vacation. I had planned to wake up and watch the sun rise with coffee—I love rooms that provide a coffeemaker, as this one does. I love the decadence of brewing a fresh cup of coffee (which I never do at home) and sitting on a balcony with my glasses still on, hair uncombed, face still lined with pillow marks, drinking coffee as the world wakes up.

Waking up is the greatest pain and the finest pleasure. I loathe waking up to the alarm clock, but here I don't need one.

Traveling alone is a leap of faith, the trust that you will be okay with no one watching out for you. The knowledge that at dinner you are an oddity, "Table for one please." Who comes to Hawaii on their own, alone, this purview of honeymooners and wedding parties and couples and families? Who arrives alone on Christmas Day? Who wears a sundress to dinner alone with sandals and a good book? The waitress chats a moment too long; she is dying to know your story—who are you? Are you someone? But there isn't a story here, just a macadamia-nut-encrusted mahimahi with a scoop of plain rice, and it is overpriced, but it's vacation. And a glass of pinot grigio—my favorite. It astonishes me how easy I am at this now, traveling alone. Two years ago I was paralyzed with fear for my first dinner alone.

The first time I ever had dinner alone (McDonalds's drive-through in the car doesn't count), I was in Seattle, I was alone, it was late, and I was starving. I was there to promote my book that has *Drunk* in the title. The restaurant hotel was a lovely place full of couples, and I had never dined alone. Ever. I grew up in a time and in a region of the country where it was unheard of for a woman to dine alone; I am not from some bygone era, an Amelia Earhart throwback wearing crimped finger waves, scandalizing society with my aviator pants. I grew up in the South, where you live with an extended network. It's not common to find women dining alone. But I was hungry. And hunger takes precedence over protocol.

That first trip, that first night alone, my author's escort was less than enchanted by me, and she left me at the hotel. I was exhausted and hungry and talked out. The restaurant's name was Lola (go there if it still exists). The waitress was kind, seated me at a private table, and gave me a taste of the potato wedges, which were not at all on my "God, don't let me be fat for the tour" diet. I had rice and some kind of meat and wine, and I took a friend's unbound manuscript with me as if I were working, and I was thanking God each moment for that little stack of papers as I looked so busy and important, making notes and using my beloved Post-it note highlighter pen. I wondered if people were staring.

After my second glass of wine that night in Seattle, I relaxed into it. A couple of people looked at me with mild interest. And it passed; they became engrossed in their own dramas and lives, and it was nothing—some girl in a black cashmere sweater and jeans sitting at a table highlighting a manuscript, drinking wine and picking at the bowl of seasoned potato skins that her under-standing server brought . . . just because.

I lived through my first dinner alone. I felt almost victorious after it, as if I had gone where women like me had never gone before. As if I had established some new outpost of independ-ence. As if I had declared dinner a solitary pleasure, sometimes, when needed.

There is something about that one dinner that stayed with me all those months. Late-night nachos in airports and room service at midnight in hotels never had the same punch as that one single dinner at Lola's in Seattle. I had dinner alone in a nice restaurant and no one treated me as a leper, and the ones who stared did so out of interest, not pity; at least, I saw it that way. I suddenly realized that it's all about *perspective*. Had I imagined myself as pathetic and lonely, their looks of mild interest would have crushed me, sent me back to the room, maudlin and wanting to watch *Sleepless in Seattle* on my iPod.

But that Post-it note pen saved me. The simple sheaf of papers—they were a manuscript, but Lord knows I could have been reading the latest cosmetic product survey off cosmo.com—made me feel purposeful. Important. No matter that I was on an actual book tour promoting a whole work of my own. The simple act of marking and revising paperwork made me feel useful; I had presence. I was busy, and clearly Someone to Be Reckoned With. I made *myself* different with just a little change of attitude.

I could dine alone and be independent.

So, fast-forward to all these months later. It's Christmas weekend on no business at all, not even pretend business (who does business at a resort on Maui anyway?), and I was in a sleepy vacation town in Hawaii having dinner at the ungodly hour of 6:00 PM. But I had my excuses for getting the early-bird special—I'd gotten up before dawn, driven the island, swam in the ocean, showered that bath of redemption that comes after sand and sun. When I arrived for dinner, the lady at the desk greeted me instantly: "You must be Room 418," she said.

"I am," I said, without a frisson of doubt.

"Just this way to your table," she said. And there I was on the patio, right beside the window for an ocean view, a glass of wine, a tiny fillet of mahimahi, and a scoop of rice; the waiter smiled, the service was neat and unobtrusive—who the heck cares why I am all alone? Maybe I'm Somebody. Maybe I am Nobody at All. But this place is so beautiful and relaxed, I don't care.

I have no apology to make. I am living my life. MY life.

Alone is a liberating, sometimes lonely, uncomplicated, very complex, infinitely powerful place to be when you choose it. I couldn't have been this woman just a few years ago. I would have made up a lie, said my boyfriend was delayed, said anything for a cover. Now I offer nothing at all personal. A smile, a warm hello, a hearty thank-you for excellent service. No one serving me food, making the bed, checking me in or out, renting me a car, needs to know anything about my life. I am not accountable to strangers.

One day maybe it will be me plus one. One day I will most likely travel again with a companion. Sometimes I have been alone, and sometimes I have had companionship this year— funny, strange, hilarious, sweet, unexpected companionship. I needed it then for whatever purpose it served. Some of my dates made me realize I was looking for qualities I had never even considered (yes, it would be nice to meet a man who knows some American history). Some of my dates were just fun, helping me be comfortable in my own skin. They may never know what they did for me. Maybe I was just a plot point in some of their own stories, they went on to meet a perfect partner, and I helped them clarify what they did and didn't want. Maybe for some of them I was just a fork in the road getting them to their right paths; it's all a mystery.

Today I am myself, as one. An individual. Maybe my life won't end with a Mr. Darcy, a true love, a holiday romance. This is not the story with the ". . . and they lived happily ever after" ending. This is the true story of me, who always thought I had to be half of something to be anything at all. My happy ending probably won't even be an end at all, just a beginning to some new bizarre, quirky story with new and strange forms of hair removal.

I am so lucky. I got the chance to see that I can be one whole woman: complete, responsible for my own happiness, responsible for my own well-being, taxes, happiness, comfort, choices, decisions—all of it. Happiness is an inside job. There is no list, no catalog from the Universe we sift through to order up a perfect life, a perfect mate, a perfect home. We make our lives. There is no perfect. There is only goofy, flawed happiness and everything in between. I can stop fretting about my unfinishedness.

We wake up each day and make it as good as it can be by deciding to see our lives as a continuum, not as a goal or a single resolution on a piece of paper. Meet a goal and it's over, on to the next goal! But a life lived for harmony, for balance, for goofiness, for jokes, for fart stories, for a bikini wax that you know will make a great story at a party—*that* is living. It's the tiny spaces in between the big goals that let me live. It's the moment I stood in line with no shame and said, "Table for one, please." It's the moment I smiled at a stranger on a train. It's the day I grabbed my camera because the cat was in a perfect ray of sunlight, all artistic and furry.

It's so simple. It's not the resolutions, the tidy endings. It's all the tangles that make up a life. A glass of wine you pour as your mom tells you about this funny thing the dog did. It's that afternoon spent making tamales with your father and he tells you something you never knew about your family.

Home is wherever you make it, whether you dine alone or dine together or sleep only on one side of the bed, leaving room for the unexpected future.

Home is where you wake up. Home is where you take pride in even the smallest thing—a zucchini you grew, the socks you made by hand, the poster board collage from a night full of laughter and glue sticks.

You take it with you. Home is everywhere you are.

Knit & Crochet
Projects

Knitting and Crocheting Abbreviation Key

beg = beginning

bpdc = back post double crochet

bl = bobble stitch

BO = bind off

ch = chain

CO = cast on

dc = double crochet

dec = decrease

DPNs = double-pointed needles

fdc = foundation double crochet

fpdc = front post double crochet

fpdc2tog = front post double crochet 2 together

fpsc = front post single crochet

hdc = half double crochet

inc = increase

K = knit

kfb = knit into the front and back of a stitch

k2tog = knit two together

lp = loop

M1 = increase one stitch, or "make one"

P = purl

p2tog = purl two together

p/u = pick up

pwise = purlwise

rep = repeat

rnd = round

RS = right side

sc = single crochet

skp = slip 1, knit 1, pass the slipped stitch over and off

sl = slip

sl st = slip stitch

ssk = slip, slip, knit

st = stitch

st st = stockinette stitch

st(s) = stitch, stitch(es)

tog = together

WS = wrong side

w/t = wrap and turn

yo = yarn over

( ) = indicates a group of stitches that are worked together

[ ] = indicates a group of stitches that should be worked together the number of times given after the brackets

Easiest Hand
(and/or Arm) Warmers Ever

❀

WHEN I FIRST LEARNED TO KNIT, I discovered I was a freakishly tight knitter. My cramped little stitches created impermeable barriers of stockinette, watertight ribbing, and bulletproof seed stitch. This was fantastic for making jokes (and scarves so stiff they could stand on their own), but it was not so great for creating wearable knits. I started knitting gauge swatches before every project. Knitting a gauge swatch lets you know if you need to go up a needle size (or three) or adjust your tension to fit the pattern.

But gauge swatches are sometimes all I knit. I admit it—I love the knitted square. What is a scarf, anyway, except a knitted square that kept going? The knitted square is portable, mindless, and can be knit up from any yarn and any combination of needles. Just one little square— it's so fast, so easy, so obtainable.

These hand warmers/arm warmers are just longish squares. They're little miniature scarves for your hands, wrists, and/or arms—perfect projects for using up small skeins of yarn. Anyone who can knit a row can knit a pair of these hand warmers in just hours—knitted flat, these are sewn together when you're done (remember to leave a hole for your thumb) and they look chic alone or worn over a pair of winter gloves. I have made nine hundred pairs of hand warmers. My hands will be toasty until the apocalypse.

Hand Warmers in 4 x 4 Ribbing

MATERIALS:

- ♦ **Yarn:** one skein Noro Silk Garden Lite
- ♦ **Needles:** one set size 7 straight needles
- ♦ **Other Tools:** one large-eye yarn needle for seaming
- ♦ **Optional:** one ice-cold beer for holding in warmed hands

INSTRUCTIONS:

Step 1: Cast on 40 stitches loosely. If you need to, cast on using a size 8 needle to get a loose cast-on edge.

Step 2: Work in a K4, P4 ribbing for the entire piece. My hand warmers are about eight inches long. Cast off, leaving a long yarn tail (you can use it for seaming).

Step 3: Thread yarn through a large-eye yarn needle and sew up the sides lengthwise, leaving a 1½-inch opening for the thumb (or less if you want).

Longish Arm Warmers in 2 x 2 Ribbing

MATERIALS:

- ♦ **Yarn:** one skein Noro Silk Garden Lite
- ♦ **Needles:** one set size 7 straight needles
- ♦ **Other Tools:** one large-eye yarn needle for seaming

INSTRUCTIONS:

Step 1: Cast on 40 stitches loosely. If you need to, cast on using a size 8 needle to get a loose cast-on edge.

Step 2: Work in a K2, P2 ribbing for the entire piece. (My arm warmers are about 12 inches long.)

Step 3: Cast off, leaving a long yarn tail (you can use it for seaming).

Step 4: Thread yarn through a large-eye yarn needle and sew up the sides lengthwise, leaving a 1½-inch opening for the thumb (or less if you want).

Voilà! Wear and be warmed.
Hold onto cold beer with your protective beer cozy.

OTHER VARIATIONS: Try these hand warmers/arm warmers in garter stitch using a hand-painted yarn—the results may surprise you. Or use a seed-stitch border on the top and bottom edges. Pick up one of those knitting books that has blanket squares and turn any square into an arm warmer with the addition of four rows of garter stitch on the top and bottom edge. Whenever I am in between projects or find a lonely single skein of yarn, I make hand warmers. Easiest project ever!

Mistake Rib Scarf

AH, THE SCARF—the finest project in all of knitting! You can wear scarves for about half an hour once a year in Los Angeles, but I keep making them for me, friends, family members, and complete strangers on the street. Scarves are beautiful and fulfilling and when made with bulky yarn, they're a short-term commitment. This is the easiest scarf pattern ever, but it looks complicated! The ridges formed from the oddly aligned knits and purls (The "mistake" in the rib) create a gorgeous fabric with no right or wrong side. Your friends will be amazed at your impressive skills.

MATERIALS:

♦ **Yarn and Needles:** Pick any soft yarn and the larger needle recommended on the ball band. (Most skeins of yarn have a wrapper—called the ball band—that tells you which size needle to use.)

INSTRUCTIONS:

Step 1: Cast on stitches in multiples of 4, plus three extra stitches (for example, using a bulky yarn and a size 11 needle, I cast on 27 stitches—that's 24 stitches plus three extra. You could cast on 15 stitches, or 23 stitches, or 31 stitches. It just has to be some number that is a multiple of 4, plus 3 extra stitches. You probably figured that out by now).

Step 2: K2, P2 all the way across the row. You'll have one unknitted stitch at the end of each row—just purl it!

Step 3: Knit in pattern until piece measures as long as you prefer for your scarves, then bind off.

Seriously, that is the whole stitch pattern.
I am not even lying to you.

Super Easy and Fast Hand-Knit Beret

❀

THIS IS THE PERFECT HAT for wearing on vacations to glamorous places. Pair it with oversized glasses and put on some lip gloss—no one will ever know your hotel room's hair dryer was broken and your curling iron melted from the electricity converter that didn't live up to its promise.

Gauge: Three stitches to the inch in the knitted stockinette portion of the hat (knit your gauge swatch using the larger-size needles). Adjust needle size to achieve gauge.

MATERIALS:

◆ Yarn: Any bulky yarn. I have used this same pattern with good results on one skein of Patons UpCountry, two skeins Lion Brand Landscapes, one and a half skeins of Jo-Ann's store-brand yarn Sensations Licorice, and one skein of Lion Brand Wool-Ease Chunky. Each hat takes about 110 yards of yarn depending on how long you make the body of the beret.

◆ Needles: Part of the reason this hat knits up so fast is that you make it on big needles! You will need a 16-inch size 10 circular needle, 16-inch size 11 circular needle, and double-pointed needles in size 11.

♦ **Other Tools:** Stitch marker, crochet hook, and large-eye needle to finish and weave in ends. Stitch markers and a large-eye yarn needle (or crochet hook) for weaving in the ends when you're done. Hearty red wine for glamorous dinners with beret.

INSTRUCTIONS:

Step 1: Cast on 52 stitches using the size 10 needle. Place a marker and join your stitches into a round. [NOTE: *To get a nicer-looking join, I have been casting on 53 stitches and then when I am ready to join stitches, I slip the 53rd stitch over to the left-hand needle and join by knitting the first two stitches on the left needle together. I'm not explaining it well, but sometimes in knitting I think you have to try something yourself before it makes any sense. Try it and see if it improves the look of your join as well.*]

Step 2: Make the ribbed brim: K1, P1 all the way around for about five rows. I prefer about an inch or an inch and a half of ribbing on my berets.

Step 3: Increase for beretlike poufiness: When you have a wide enough ribbed brim for your liking, begin making the increase row. Still using the size 10 needle, increase in the following way all the way around the hat: K1, M1 (kfb); repeat across row.

(If Step 3 made no sense to you, it's because it was written in knitting shorthand, a mysterious secret language. Really it just means: Knit 1, then make 1 by knitting into the front and back of the next stitch, then repeat across row).

Step 4: The even longer explanation: On Stitch no. 1, you knit the stitch. Just knit it like normal. On Stitch no. 2, you knit into the front of the stitch. Then, instead of dropping it off the left needle, you leave it on the left needle and now knit it again through the back loop—yes, the *back loop of the exact same stitch you just knit into.* Now, you finally drop it off the left needle. In this way you have made two stitches where before there was only one.

Step 5: Next stitch: You simply knit it.

Step 6: The stitch after that: You do the increasing thing again, making an extra stitch where before there was only one. Therefore, you increase on every OTHER stitch. That creates 26 brand-new stitches. Magic! At the end of the row you should have a total of 78 stitches.

MAKE THE BODY OF THE BERET:

Step 7: Now, switch to your size 11 circular needle. It's easy to switch—just start knitting with your size 11 (16-inch) circular needle. The rest of the hat is done in plain old stockinette, so in the round that means you knit every stitch. Knit until the stockinette body of the hat measures about 4½ inches tall. When the body of the hat is about 4½–5 inches tall, begin decreases as instructed in Step 9.

Step 8: K11, k2tog. Do this all the way across the row.
[NOTE: I always place a marker right after my k2tog because after that I never even have to count to know I am decreasing in the right place. With a marker you just always know to knit the two stitches together right before each stitch marker. I also use different markers from the one

that designates the end of the row (where you initially joined up the stitches). That way I know what is marking decreases is different from what is designating the end of the row. I am all about making my knitting so simple I can do it while watching TV and drinking wine, which in my world is some fierce multitasking.]

Step 9: Knit one row with no decreasing.

K10, k2tog. Repeat all the way across the row.

Knit one row with no decreasing.

K9, k2tog. Repeat all the way across the row.

Knit one row with no decreasing.

K8, k2tog. Repeat all the way across the row.

Knit one row with no decreasing.

K7, k2tog . . .

And so on. Switch to your double-pointed needles when the circular needle gets awkward. Knit until you only have a few stitches on your needles (I usually knit down to the bitter end, but with this hat, it's best to end the hat when you're down to about 12 stitches so you don't get a weird pointy bit). Cut the yarn and leave a long yarn tail.

FINISHING INSTRUCTIONS:

Using your large-eye yarn needle, thread the yarn tail through it and then bring the yarn all the way through the stitches to close the beret. I usually do this twice because I am paranoid. Then finish it with a knot (ha! Yes, there are knots in knitting!) and weave in the ends. Wear on exotic vacation or to grocery store.

Reversible Halloweenie Beanie

THIS PATTERN WAS CREATED primarily because I thought it was funny. I know the world is full of knitters who inspire, or make lovely works of art, or create functional and useful items. I make stuff up because I think it is funny and has the potential to make me laugh while stuck in traffic, which is exactly how the Halloweenie Beanie got started.

Gauge: I'm getting 4 stitches to the inch on the beanie. The stem's gauge isn't crucial. It's a stem, all organic and free-form.

MATERIALS:

♦ **Yarn:** 1¼ skeins Mission Falls Superwash Wool in orange. For the pumpkin's stem, I used a small amount of Lion Brand Wool-Ease in a pretty heathered green color. I had the green left over from a scarf I made a hundred years ago. This pattern took a little more than one skein of orange and a very small amount of green.

♦ **Needles:** With my SupraTight Knitting Superpowers, I went up a recommended needle size and used a size 9 circular needle (16-inch circular) for most of the hat and switched to size 9 double-pointed needles when needed during decreasing. Normal knitters will want to use size 8 (16-inch circular) needles or else this hat will be way too big. For the pumpkin stem, you'll need a set of size 10 or 10.5 straight needles.

♦ **Other Tools:** Stitch marker, crochet hook, and large-eye needle to finish and weave in ends. Cat helper, sense of humor, and wine recommended but not necessary.

INSTRUCTIONS FOR THE BEANIE:

Step 1: On circular needles, cast on 88 stitches in orange yarn and join to knit in the round. Place stitch marker at start of round.

Step 2: K4, P4 all the way around to create a ribbed edge. I did this for a little more than an inch, or about five rows.

Step 3: For the body, the hat is basically stockinette with a single rib every 8 stitches. So you will K7, P1 all the way around for the entire body until hat measures 6 inches from base, including rib.

Step 4: The reason this hat is reversible is because when you begin decreasing, rather than knitting 2 stitches together (as I have in all my other hats), here I decided to purl 2 stitches together, which creates a decrease ridge that perfectly lines up with the purl ridges on the reverse stockinette side of the hat.

Step 5: Start decreasing by knitting 6 stitches, purling 2 stitches together, and repeating all the way around the row.

Step 6: For all the remaining rows, you'll knit until you see that purl stitch coming—you'll see it—and then purl together the plain stitch before it plus the lone purl stitch. Or, if that's too confusing, just follow this instruction:

> K6, p2tog
> K5, p2tog

K4, p2tog

K3, p2tog

K2, p2tog

Step 7: Switch to DPNs when there are too few stitches to fit around the circular needle. *[NOTE: I found this to be the easiest hat to decrease of all the hats I've made—you don't need to count to know when to decrease, just look for that purl ridge in your stockinette and you're ready to decrease. Decreasing purlwise (fancypants way of saying "purl two together") is very easy and it prepares you for the pumpkin's stem, which has a lot of freaking purling.]*

Step 8: Thread large-eye needle through stitches and remove from needles. Stitch down through top of hat to secure and keep from unraveling. Finish and weave in ends.

INSTRUCTIONS FOR CREATING THE PUMPKIN'S CURLICUE STEM:

Step 1: Cast on 18 stitches. I used a size 10.5 straight needle; you may want to use a size 10. CAST ON LOOSELY. SERIOUSLY.

Step 2: Knit into the front, back, and front again of each stitch before dropping it off the left needle. Just keep in mind that for this project, you knit each stitch three times—once in front, once through the back loop, and finally through the front again. That's why it's *muy importante* to cast on loosely.

Step 3: Bind off all stitches purlwise. That just means you bring your yarn to the front, purl the first stitch, purl the next stitch, then pass the first stitch over the second like a regular bind off. I find that binding off purlwise is a lot more time-consuming, but it's necessary for this project.

And voilà! You have a stem! This is an easy way to create a knitted curlicue. Or you can always just add a pom-pom if the curly stem is a tad much for you.

Happy Halloweenie Beanie!

Quick Knit Date-Night Bag

BY MYRA WOOD

EVEN IF THE DATE ISN'T MEMORABLE, this little bag will be. It's small enough to do double duty as a cosmetics bag—that's how I use mine. It holds my lipstick, powder, and mascara safely together inside my behemoth nine-hundred-pound handbag.

Gauge: 3 sts x 5 rows + 1 inch

MATERIALS:

♦ **Yarn:** one skein Lion Brand Jiffy black; one skein Plymouth Eros Glitz (or any two yarns held together throughout that match gauge); one skein gold Lion Brand Lamé.

♦ **Needles:** Size 9 U.S. needles; size G crochet hook

♦ **Fabric:** ½ yard for lining

♦ **Accessories:** Snap bag closure, large button for center of flowers, Fabri-Tac glue (or other fabric glue of your choice)

♦ **Optional:** Beads or other suitable material for strap

SPECIAL ABBREVIATIONS USED IN THIS PATTERN:

p/u = pick up

skp = slip 1, knit 1, pass the slipped stitch over and off

ssk = slip, slip, knit

w/t = wrap and turn

INSTRUCTIONS:

Holding 1 stand of each yarn together, CO 20 sts

Front:

Row 1: K

Row 2: and all even rows to Row 24: P.

Row 3: Kfb, knit to last 2 sts, kfb (22 sts)

Row 5: K

Row 7: K

Row 9: Kfb, knit to last 2 sts, kfb (24 sts)

Row 11: K

Row 13: K

Row 15: Kfb, knit to last 2 sts, kfb (26 sts)

Row 17: K

Row 19: K

Row 21: Kfb, knit to last 2 sts, kfb (28 sts)

Bottom:

Row 23: K23, w/t

Row 24: P19, w/t

Row 25: K16, w/t

Row 26: P13, w/t

Row 27: K10, w/t

Row 28: P7, w/t

Row 29: K across, p/u wraps

Row 30: Purl across, p/u wraps

Back:

Row 31: Skp, K to last 2 sts, k2tog (26 sts)

Row 32: and remaining even rows: Purl.

Row 33: K

Row 35: K

Row 37: Skp, K to last 2 sts, k2tog (24 sts)

Row 39: K

Row 41: K

Row 43: Skp, k to last 2 sts, k2tog (22 sts)

Row 45: K

Row 47: K

Row 49: Skp, k to last 2 sts, k2tog (20 sts)

Row 51: K

Row 53: Mark edge of knitting with safety pin, K across.

Flap:

Row 55: Ssk, K to last 2 sts, k2tog (18 sts)

Row 57: K

Row 55: Ssk, K to last 2 sts, k2tog. (16 sts)

Row 57: K

Row 55: Ssk, K to last 2 sts, k2tog (14 sts)

Row 57: K

Row 67: Bind off as follows: Skp, return st to left needle. * k2tog loosely, return st to left needle. Rep from * to last st, cut yarn and pull through. Weave in end.

Assembly: Block very lightly to straighten edges. Cut fabric to ½ inch larger than bag shape, fold under edges and iron. Use Fabri-Tac or other glue to adhere lining to wrong side of bag. After it dries, with right sides together, fold bottom edge of bag to match safety pin where flap starts. Seam edge with whipstitch on both sides. Turn to right side. Single crochet around open edge and flap.

Large Flowers:

Cast on 10 sts with one strand of Lion Brand Jiffy black.

Row 1: Kfb all sts (20 sts)

Row 2: Kfb all sts (40 sts)

Bind off all stitches loosely. Edge with single crochet.

Small Flowers:

Cast on 6 sts with yarn A only

Row 1: Kfb all sts (12 sts)

Row 2: Kfb all sts (24 sts)

Bind off all stitches loosely.

Finishing:

Edge with single crochet. Sew flowers and snap to bag. Attach strap as desired.

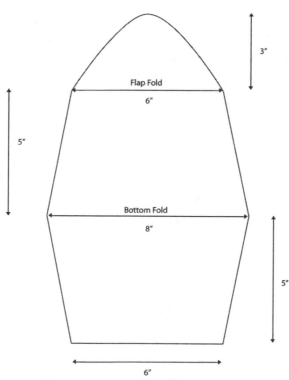

About the Designer

Myra Wood is an internationally known teacher, fiber and bead artist, designer, and author. She teaches workshops and lectures on crochet, knitting, beading, and embroidery, specializing in all things free-form at national retreats, conventions, and yarn shops across the country. Her unique beaded jewelry and knit/crochet patterns have also been featured in a wide range of publications. Myra has been crocheting, sewing, and crafting since she was young and is passionate about any opportunity to inspire others creatively. Galleries of her work can be seen at www.myrawood.com.

Island Beach Bag

BY MARTY MILLER, A.K.A. THE CROCHET DOCTOR

AVID YARN LOVERS WHO LIVE in warm climates usually have to pretend that 72 degrees is a cold spell so they can use all their cozy handmade stuff. This crocheted beach bag is made for hot weather and cold drinks! It's quick and easy to make and folds up very small but expands to hold a towel, sunscreen, trashy book, and snacks. Of course, you can use this bag for other things—school supplies, groceries, yarn, laundry—but unlike all those scarves and mittens, you can use it year-round in any climate.

Skill Level: Easy

Gauge: First 6 rounds = 4 inches

Finished Measurements: Approximately 14½ inches across by 17 inches tall

MATERIALS:

- **Yarn:** Worsted weight cotton yarn, approximately 300–400 yards
- **Crochet Hook:** US H-8 (5.00mm) or size required for gauge
- **Other Tools:** Yarn needle

ABBREVIATIONS OF SPECIAL STITCHES USED IN THIS PATTERN:

fdc = foundation double crochet

lp = loop

rnd = round

yo = yarn over

INSTRUCTIONS:

Step 1: Ch 4, yo, insert hook into first ch, yo, draw hook through st, ch 1, yo, draw hook through 2 loops, yo, draw hook through the last 2 loops. One foundation double crochet (fdc) made. (What you are doing is this: You are making a regular dc, BUT, after you bring the hook through the stitch, before you finish the dc, you are adding a ch st, and then finishing the dc.)

Step 2: Now the second stitch: yo, put your hook through the ch stitch that you made doing the first fdc. Yo, draw hook through st, ch 1, yo, draw hook through two loops, yo, draw hook through last two loops. You just made another foundation double crochet! Continue in this manner until you have the necessary number of fdcs, including the first ch 4 as one fdc stitch.

NOTES: Ch. 3 at beginning of rnd counts as dc. Ch. 4 at beginning of rnd counts as (dc, ch 1 space). You will be working on the RS of the bag, in rounds, from the bottom of the bag to the top. Join each round with a sl st, but do not turn at the end of the rounds.

INSTRUCTIONS:

Bag: Ch 4.

Rnd 1: 11 dc in 4th ch from hook. Join with sl st to top ch of beg ch. Do not turn. (12 dc)

Rnd 2: Ch 4. Skip joining, (dc, ch 1) in each dc around. Join with sl st to 3rd ch of beg ch-4. (12 [dc, ch-1] sps)

Rnd 3: Ch 3. Dc in same st as joining, dc in next ch-1 sp, *2 dc in next dc, dc in next ch-1 sp. Repeat from * around. Join with sl st to top ch of beg ch-3. (36 dc)

Rnd 4: Ch 4. Skip joining. (Dc, ch 1) in next dc, skip one dc, *[(dc, ch 1) in next dc] 2 times, skip one dc. Repeat from * around. Join with sl st to 3rd ch of beg ch-4. (24 [dc, ch-1] sps)

Rnd 5: Ch 3. Dc in same st as joining. Dc in next ch-1 sp, dc in next dc, dc in next ch-1 sp, *(2 dc in next dc, dc in next ch-1 sp, dc in next dc, dc in next ch-1 sp). Repeat from * around. Join with sl st to top ch of beg ch-3. (60 dc)

Rnd 6: Ch 4. Skip joining. (Dc, ch 1) in next dc. Skip one dc. (Dc, ch 1) in next dc, skip 1 dc. *[(dc, ch 1) in next dc] 2 times, skip 1 dc, (dc, ch 1) in next dc, skip 1 dc. Repeat from * around. Join with sl st in 3rd ch of beg ch-4. ([36 dc, ch-1] sps)

Rnd 7: Ch 3, dc in same st as joining, (dc in next ch-1 sp, dc in next dc) 2 times, dc in next ch-1 sp, *[2dc in next dc, (dc in next ch-1 sp, dc in next dc,) 2 times, dc in next ch-1 sp]. Repeat from * around. Join with sl st to top of beg ch-3. (84 dc)

Rnd 8: Ch 4, skip joining, (dc, ch 1) in next dc, skip 1 dc, [(dc, ch 1) in next dc] 2 times, *[(dc, ch 1) in next dc] 2 times. Skip 1 dc. [(dc, ch 1) in next dc. skip 1 dc] 2 times. Repeat from *around. Join with sl st in 3rd ch of beg ch-4. ([48 dc, ch-1] sps)

Rnd 9: Ch 3, dc in same st as joining, dc in ch-1 sp (dc in next dc, dc in ch-1 sp) 3 times, *2 dc in next dc, dc in ch-1 sp, (dc in next dc, dc in ch-1 sp) 3 times. Repeat from * around. Join with sl st to top of beg ch-3. (108 dc)

Rnd 10: Ch 4. Skip joining and next dc, *(dc, ch1) in next dc, skip one dc. Repeat from * around. Join with sl st in 3rd ch of beg ch-4. ([48 dc, ch-1] sps)

Rnd 11: Ch 3, skip joining. Dc in each ch-1 sp and dc around. Join with sl st to top of beg ch-3. (108 dc)

Rnds 12–27: Repeat rnds 10 and 11.

Rnd 28: Ch 1. Sc in each dc around. Join with sl st to first sc. (108 sc)

Rnd 29: Ch 1. Sc in each sc around. Join with sl st to first sc. End off.

DRAWSTRING HANDLES: MAKE 2.

Step 1: Work 150 fdc. End off.

Step 2: Weave in all ends.

Step 3: Weave each drawstring handle through one half of rnd 26. Tie ends together with an overhand knot. Fill bag with all the necessities for a day at the beach and break it in with a little sand and sunshine.

About the Designer:

Marty Miller is a crochet designer, teacher, editor, and tech editor, currently serving as the vice president of the board of directors of the Crochet Guild of America (CGOA). She teaches at the CGOA conferences and at her local yarn shop, and presents workshops throughout the country. Ever since she was five years old, when her grandmother taught her how to crochet, Marty has been passionate about crochet, and knows that a day without crochet is a day without sunshine. She has her own pattern line, Emerald Isle Designs (see www.emeraldisledesignsnc.com). For more information about Marty and her crochet, you can follow her online at http://thecrochetdoctor. blogspot.com and http://notyourgrannyscrochet.blogspot.com.

Braided I-Cord Kitchen Rug

BY COURTNEY MILLER-CALLIHAN

THIS SMALL RUG, inspired by traditional braided rag rugs, is a super-cute way to brighten up your kitchen or bath. It's also a perfect stash-busting project! All those half skeins of yarn in your stash can come together for one unified purpose: keeping the floor bright and cozy. And if you've been looking for a reason to buy a cord-making machine, this project is your excuse.

Gauge: not important for this project. The size of your rug will depend on how long you make each i-cord. The more i-cord you make, the bigger the rug!

MATERIALS:

♦ Yarn: Approximately 18 ounces of sport, DK, or worsted-weight yarns (cotton and acrylic are both good choices for this project). It helps if all of the yarns are roughly the same weight. I used Red Heart Super Soft, Plymouth Wildflower DK, Lion Brand Microspun, Lion Brand Baby Soft, and various other odds and ends from my stash.

♦ Needles: A set of double-pointed needles in a size appropriate for your chosen yarn weight (between a U.S. 4 and a U.S. 8), or a cord-making machine, like the Cool Corder, available online and at craft stores. (I bought one of these just for this project and it was a huge time-saver.)

♦ **Other Tools:** sewing needle and upholstery thread in a neutral color

INSTRUCTIONS:

Step 1: Make i-cords. Using a DPN, cast on 4 stitches. Make i-cord by knitting across all stitches using a second DPN, then pushing the stitches back to the right side of your needle and knitting across the same way again. Your yarn should be held behind the work; as you start a new "row," knit tightly so that the leftmost stitch and the rightmost stitch begin to pull together to form a tube. Continue in this way until you run out of yarn, then thread yarn through all 4 stitches, pull tight, and fasten off.

Step 2: Make two more i-cords in different colors.

Step 3: Braid i-cords together.

Step 4: Hold all three i-cords together and using a bit of upholstery thread, sew all three edges very close to one end. Knot the thread off tightly.

Step 5: Begin braiding your cords together. Keep braiding until one of your cords runs out. Hold the ends of the braid together using a rubber band. [*NOTE: I found the braiding went much more easily when I wound each cord into a center pull ball. Much more manageable!]*

Step 6: When one of your cords runs out, you can make another i-cord in a different color and add it to the rug by sewing the ends together, tip to tip, using upholstery thread as you did before. If your thread is pretty neutral in color, you don't need to worry about making your stitches too neat. It won't show!

Step 7: Keep adding more cord and braiding as before, until all of your yarn has been added. Just put a rubber band around the end of the braid for now; you'll finish it off more neatly later. At this point you should have one REALLY LONG braid of multicolored i-cord.

SHAPE THE RUG:

Step 1: Starting at the beginning of the braid, lay a piece between 6 inches and 18 inches in length on a flat surface. (This length will determine the approximate shape of your finished rug. For a rounder rug, choose a shorter length; for a longer oval, choose a longer length.) Lay another section the same length next to the first. Press the braid flat with your fingers so you can see all three colors throughout, paying special attention to the "switchback." Begin sewing the edges together using upholstery thread. Again, your stitches don't have to be very neat, but pull the thread tightly as you go, so there are no gaps between the braids.

Step 2: Keep sewing around in a spiral in this fashion, being careful to always keep the braids flat. Don't twist, or the rug will be very uncomfortable to walk on! Be generous when you are adding a new length of braid: remember that each new coil you add to the rug needs to be significantly larger than the one before, or the rug won't lay flat.

Step 3: Once you've sewn up all of your braid, sew the rubber-banded ends together as you did at the beginning, weaving in ends as necessary. Tuck this end under and tack in place on the wrong side of the rug.

Invite strangers over to admire your handmade rug, charge admission, make visitors wear little surgical booties over their feet before they can walk on its braided backside. It's a masterpiece!

About the designer:

Courtney Miller-Callihan lives and works in New York City, where her yarn provides good insulation during the winter months. She is always trying to think of new uses for scrap yarn.

Felted Wine-Bottle Cozy

❀

THIS PATTERN WAS A HAPPY ACCIDENT. It began life as an ill-fated first attempt at making hand-knit leg warmers. I picked a lovely soy/wool blend yarn that made gorgeous stripes when knitted, and I got started on what was sure to be a revival of '80s high fashion. Knitting the leg warmer was a breeze! However, I seriously miscalculated how much my calves would widen visually when covered in big horizontal stripes. I finished my first leg warmer, pulled it on over my jeans, and sashayed over to the mirror only to discover my leg had quadrupled in width with the addition of a bright orange-and-rust striped piece of knitting. I think I let out a little scream.

This project was relegated to the bottom of my sock drawer, and there it rested for months until I dug it out one day and threw it into the wash. Who knows what unique felted creation could come forth from a lonely spurned leg warmer!

Gauge: not critical for this, but before felting, I had 4 stitches to the inch.

MATERIALS:

♦ **Yarn:** 1 to 1½ skeins Patons SWS yarn. I used Natural Crimson (or you can use any feltable 100-percent wool bulky yarn). Patons

Soy Wool Stripes (SWS) felts like magic, and after two rounds in hot water, I had the perfect little wine-bottle cozy. I went from *Flashdance* Tragedy to Certified Merlot Decorator in two easy wash and rinse cycles.

♦ **Needles:** One size 10 (16-inch) circular needle

♦ **Other Tools:** One large-eye yarn needle for sewing in the ends

INSTRUCTIONS:

Step 1: Cast on 68 stitches of Patons SWS using a size 10 (16-inch) circular needle. Join stitches to knit in the round. Kind of like making a hat!

Step 2: Work in K2, P2 ribbing for 2½ inches to create a top cuff. Switch to stockinette (that's knitting every stitch since you are working in the round).

Step 3: Work in stockinette in the round for as long as you can stand it. I worked for 13½ inches.

Step 4: Finish off with another 2½ inches of K2, P2 ribbing for the cuff on the other end.

Step 5: If you have skinnier legs than me, you might be able to use this pattern for leg warmers, except this sucker will probably fall off your skinny calves in about two seconds flat. Whoops! But then again, yay! You and your skinny legs! To make this leg warmer into a wine warmer, you'll want to felt it in the washing machine.

FELTING INSTRUCTIONS:

Place the knitted piece into a pillowcase and secure the top of the pillowcase with a rubber band. Or you can use a zippered pillowcase (I think that's easier). The pillowcase keeps the fuzz and yarn bits from clogging up your machine. Put the closed pillowcase in the washer with a few pairs of heavy denim jeans. I like to use denim because it doesn't give off lint like towels do. Add washing detergent and set your machine to permanent press or heavy wash using the hottest water setting.

Felting results vary depending on your machine, your water temperature, the soap you use—even the mineral composition of your water can alter the felting magic. You may want to take your cozy out before the spin cycle and check on it—depending on the strength of your machine and the alignment of the planets, you might be done already. And letting a piece run through the spin cycle can create permanent creasing. But I just threw caution to the wind and let the cozy run through the whole cycle. If it hasn't felted enough (if you can still see a lot of stitch definition), run it through the machine again.

When it's felted enough for your liking, shape over a wine bottle and let air dry. If the top of the bag isn't fitted enough for the bottle, fold down the cuff and use a ribbon or tie to draw it together snugly. Break dancing optional.

Retro Crochet Toilet-Seat Cover and Matching Toilet-Paper Cozy

BY DREW EMBORSKY, A.K.A. THE CROCHET DUDE

NOTHING SAYS 1972 LIKE a dainty handmade cozy for your toilet-seat lid. There is an entire generation of Americans who grew up in homes where the toilet lid was more elaborately dressed than the kids, and the toilet paper was cleverly hidden beneath something made of yarn (and sometimes dime-store Barbie knockoffs). This retro bathroom set will take you right back to the Age of Macramé.

Gauge: 11 sts x 9 rows = 4 inches in fpdc

Size: fits average-size toilet seat

Finished Measurements: 14 inches wide by 17 inches long

MATERIALS:

♦ **Yarn:** Worsted-weight kitchen cotton, 6 oz beige; 3 oz green; 1 oz blue

♦ **Needles:** Crochet hook U.S. I/9 (5.5mm) or size required for gauge

SPECIAL STITCHES USED IN THIS PATTERN:

Front post double crochet (fpdc): Yarn over, insert hook from front to back to front around post of stitch, yarn over, pull up loop, (yarn over, pull through two loops on hook) two times.

Back post double crochet (bpdc): Yarn over, insert hook from back to front to back around post of stitch, yarn over, pull up loop, (yarn over, pull through two loops on hook) two times.

Front post single crochet (fpsc): insert hook from front to back to front around post of stitch, yarn over, pull up loop, yarn over, pull through two loops on hook.

Front post double crochet 2 together (fpdc2tog): *Yarn over, insert hook from back to front around post of next stitch, yarn over, pull up loop, yarn over, pull through two loops on hook. Repeat from *one more time. Yarn over, pull through all loops on hook.

[NOTE: The beige part of the project is worked entirely on the wrong side, and then coordinating colors are added to the right side of the project.]

INSTRUCTIONS:

Rnd 1: (WS) Ch 4, 11 dc in fourth ch from hook. Do not join rounds, use stitch marker to indicate the beg of each rnd (12 sts counting beg ch 3)

Rnd 2: 2 fpdc around each dc (24 sts).

Rnd 3: * Fpdc around next st, 2 fpdc around next st, rep from * around (36 sts).

Rnd 4: *Fpdc around each of next 2 sts, 2 fpdc around next st, rep from * around (48 sts).

Rnd 5: * Fpdc around each of next 3 sts, 2 fpdc around next st, rep from * around (60 sts).

Rnd 6: * Fpdc around each of next 4 sts, 2 fpdc around next st, rep from * around (72 sts).

Rnd 7: * Fpdc around each of next 5 sts, 2 fpdc around next st, rep from * around (84 sts).

Rnd 8: * Fpdc around each of next 6 sts, 2 fpdc around next st, rep from * around (96 sts).

Rnd 9: * [Fpsc around each of next 7 sts, 2 fpsc around next st] three times, [fpdc around each of next 7 sts, 2 fpdc around next st] three times, rep from * once more (108 sts).

Rnd 10: * [Fpsc around each of next 8 sts, 2 fpdc around next st] three times, [fpdc around each of next 8 sts, 2 fpdc around next st] three times, rep from * once more (120 sts).

Rnd 11: * [Fpsc around each of next 9 sts, 2 fpdc around next st] three times, [fpdc around each of next 9 sts, 2 fpdc around next st] three times, rep from * once more (132 sts).

Rnd 12: * [Fpsc around each of next 10 sts, 2 fpdc around next st] 3 times, [fpdc around each of next 10 sts, 2 fpdc around next st] three times, rep from * once more (144 sts).

Rnd 13: * Fpdc around each of next 11 sts, 2 fpdc around next st, rep from * around (156 sts).

Rnd 14: * Fpdc around each of next 12 sts, 2 fpdc around next st, rep from * around (168 sts).

Rnd 15: * Fpdc around each of next 13 sts, 2 fpdc around next st, rep from * around (180 sts).

Rnds 16–17: Fpdc around each st. At end of Rnd 17 tie a scrap piece of yarn around last st of round (180 sts).

Rnd 18: Fpdc2tog around (90 sts).

Rnd 19: * Fpdc around next st, bpdc around next st, rep from * around. At end of rnd, sl st to first st to join. Fasten off.

Turn inside out to RS.

Rnd 1: (RS) With green, attach with an sc to back loop of stitch at marker placed on Rnd 17, ch 1, * sc in back loop of next st, ch 1. Rep from * around. Do not join at end of round.

Rnds 2–9: *sc in back loop of next st, ch 1. Rep from * around. At end of rnd 9, sc in next st. Fasten off

Rnd 10: With blue, attach with a sc to back loop of next st, ch 1, * sc in next st, ch 1. Rep from * around. Sl st to first blue st of rnd to join. Fasten off.

Weave in all ends.

Toilet Paper Cozy

With beige:

Rnd 1: (WS) Ch 4, 11 dc in 4th ch from hook. Do not join rounds, use stitch marker to indicate the beg of each rnd (12 sts counting beg ch 3)

Rnd 2: 2 fpdc around each dc (24 sts).

Rnd 3: * Fpdc around next st, 2 fpdc around next st, rep from * around (36 sts).

Rnd 4: * Fpdc around each of next 2 sts, 2 fpdc around next st, rep from * around (48 sts).

Rnds 5–12: Fpdc around ea st (48 sts).

Fasten off beige and attach green.

Rnds 13–15: Fpdc around ea st (48 sts).

Fasten off green, attach blue

Rnd 16: Fpdc around each st (48 sts).

Fasten off blue.

Weave in all ends.

About the Designer

Drew Emborsky's quirky title as "The Crochet Dude" and his kitschy tongue-in-cheek designs have propelled him from a young, unknown fiber artist to the cutting edge of the fiber design world. His unique role as a male knitter and crocheter has opened doors for other men who were stuck in the closet with their yarn, knitting needles, and crochet hooks. Drew studied fine art at Kendall College of Art and Design in Grand Rapids, Michigan, and is an associate professional member of the Crochet Guild of America, where he received a master certificate in crochet. Emborsky is the author of *The Crochet Dude's Designs for Guys: 30 Projects Men Will Love* and has his own line of pattern books for Leisure Arts. He lives in Houston, Texas, and writes about his life and designs at www.thecrochetdude.com.

Flip-Flop Coaster

BY DREW EMBORSKY, THE CROCHET DUDE

❀

THESE SUMMER-INSPIRED COASTERS fit perfectly over the base and stem of a wine glass like a pair of comfy poolside flip-flops. Make them in different colors and you can hide your germaphobia in style— everyone at the party gets their own coaster and they serve as personalized beverage tags so you don't accidentally swill after a stranger.

MATERIALS:

♦ **Yarn:** Small amount of kitchen cotton yarn (such as Lion Cotton Yarn, Sugar 'n Cream Cotton Yarn, etc.) in two colors

♦ **Needles:** Crochet hook size G/6 (4.25 mm)

COASTER INSTRUCTIONS:

Rnd 1: Ch 3, 8 sc in 3 ch from hook (do not join rounds; use a scrap piece of yarn to mark beginning of rows).

Rnd 2: (2 sc in next stitch) three times, (2 hdc in next st) twice, (2 sc in next stitch) 3 times (16 stitches).

Rnd 3: (2 sc in next stitch, sc in following stitch) three times, (2 hdc in next stitch, hdc in following stitch) twice, (2 sc in next stitch, sc in following stitch) three times (24 stitches).

Rnd 4: (2 sc in next stitch, sc in the next 2 stitches) three times, (2 hdc in next stitch, hdc in the next 2 stitches) twice, (2 sc in next stitch, sc in the next 2 stitches) three times (32 stitches).

Rnd 5: (2 sc in next stitch, sc in the next 3 stitches) three times, (2 hdc in next stitch, hdc in the next 3 stitches) twice, (2 sc in next stitch, sc in the next 3 stitches) three times. Place marker around 5th, 19th, and 32nd stitch of each round (40 stitches).

Rnd 6: (2 sc in next stitch, sc in the next 4 stitches) three times, (2 hdc in next stitch, hdc in the next 4 stitches) twice, (2 sc in next stitch, sc in the next 4 stitches) three times. Slip stitch, fasten off (48 stitches).

STRAP INSTRUCTIONS:

Step 1: With contrasting color, attach with a single crochet in first stitch marked in Rnd 5, sc in next stitch of Rnd 5. Ch 10, sc in next stitch marked in Rnd 5, Ch 10, sc in last stitch marked in Rnd 5, sc in next stitch of Rnd 5.

Step 2: Next row: Ch 1, turn, sc in first two stitches, sc in every other ch, sc in next sc, sc in every other ch, sc in last two sc. Fasten off, weave in ends. **Put a wineglass on the coaster and enjoy!**

Brain Freeze Ice-Cream Cozy

BY DREW EMBORSKY, THE CROCHET DUDE

❀

KEEP YOUR HANDS FROM FREEZING while you have a little late-night ice cream. It's much more attractive than wearing mittens to eat a pint of Chubby Hubby.

Gauge: 15 sts x 16 rows = 4 inches (10 cm) in sc

Finished Size: Fits pint-size ice-cream container; 7½-inch circumference by 2¾ inches tall

MATERIALS:

- ◆ **Yarn:** Small amount of worsted-weight cotton in three colors
- ◆ **Needles:** Crochet hook size I/9 (5.5mm)
- ◆ **Dessert Selection:** Pint of ice cream
- ◆ **Accessories:** Spoon

Special Stitch: Bobble (bl)—insert hook in st indicated, yo pull up loop, ch 3, yo pull through both loops on hook.

INSTRUCTIONS:

With Color A, ch 38, join with an sl st to first ch, being sure not to twist ch.

Rnd 1: Ch 2 (counts as first st now and throughout), dc in each st around, join with an sl st to top of beg ch 2. (38 sts)

Rnd 2: Ch 2, fpdc, (bpdc, fpdc) around, join with an sl st to top of beg ch 2, fasten off.

With Color B

Rnd 3: Join with a sc to bl of any st, sc in bl of each st around, join with an sl st to first sc.

Rnd 4: Ch 1, sc in same st, bl, (sc, bl) around, join with an sl st to first sc.

Rnd 5: Ch 1, sc in same st, sc in each st around, join with an sl st to first sc, fasten off.

With Color C

Rnd 6: Join with an sl st to bl of any st, ch 2, dc in bl of each st around, join with an sl st to top of beg ch 2.

Rnd 7: Ch 2, fpdc, (bpdc, fpdc) around, join with an sl, st to top of beg ch 2, fasten off.

Weave in all ends, insert pint of ice cream, use spoon to enjoy the creamy goodness.

Lonely Hearts
Personal Massager Cozy

BY LUCIA HICKS

❀

THIS PATTERN GIVES YOU the perfect place to store your personal massager, and it's decorated with a deceptively sweet heart motif. Of course, you can size it to fit your iPhone, your remote control, or whatever battery-operated device strikes your fancy.

Gauge: 5 sts and 6 rows = 1 inch in stranded pattern

MATERIALS:

♦ Yarn: worsted-weight yarn, one 50-gram ball each of colors A (red) and B (white); any fiber content is fine as long as the yarn is durable and won't stretch much. Waste yarn of a different color and slightly thinner than working yarn would work.

♦ Needles: One set DPNs, U.S. size 7 or size needed to give gauge; one U.S. size G crochet hook

INSTRUCTIONS:

Step 1: With waste yarn make a crochet chain of 20 or so loops, marking the end because you will be unraveling it from the end later. One side of the chain will have a series of loops, and the other will have loops with a little bump in the middle of each loop.

Step 2: With yarn color A, pick up 19 sts through the little bumps. Purl across the row.

Step 3: Begin short rows.

Row 1: Turn and knit across to the last st. Instead of knitting the last st, move the yarn to the front and wrap it around the st to the back, keeping the st on the left needle, which will become the right needle as you turn the work. [*NOTE: All of your wraps will go from the knit side to the purl side.*]

Row 2: Beginning with the first st on the left needle, which is the second st of the row (because you wrapped the first st of the row, and it's already on the right needle), purl to the last st, move the yarn to the back and wrap it around to the front, keeping the st on the left needle.

Row 3: Beginning with the second st of the row, knit to the second-to-last st, wrap and turn.

Row 4: Beginning with the third st of the row, purl to the second-to-last st, wrap and turn. Continue in this way until you have four sts wrapped on each side.

Step 4: Now begin the second half of the short rows, which some people call the long rows.

Row 1: Beginning with the first unwrapped st, knit to the first wrapped st at the other end, and knit the st and the wrap together. (To make this easier, I slip the st to the right needle and use the left needle to lift the wrap onto the needle, then slip the st and wrap(s) back before knitting them together.) Put a second wrap around the next st.

Row 2: Turn and purl the st you just reactivated and continue across the row to the nearest wrapped st. Purl the st and the wrap together (to make the two short-row angles look the same, I work all my purl pickups through the back loop). Put a second wrap around the next st.

Step 5: Repeat rows 1 and 2 until all sts are active again, not forgetting to pick up the wraps on the end sts. These 19 sts will be the front of the cozy.

Step 6: Now unfasten the base crochet chain from the end and unravel it from the cast-on sts, picking the live stitches up onto another needle as you go. There will be one st that isn't really a st but a backward loop; pick this up as well so that you pick up a total of 19 sts. These 19 sts will be the back of the cozy.

Step 7: Arrange the sts on three or four DPNs. You should have the front sts separate from the back sts.

Step 8: Work one round even, picking up a st if necessary to close the gaps between original and picked-up sts. Decrease to compensate for picked-up sts.

Step 9: With color B, work one round even.

Step 10: Begin the stranded color pattern, working each row shown on the chart once on the front sts and again on the back sts. *(NOTE: The chart includes one plain color B round before the stranded pattern*

and another plain color B round after the stranded pattern.)
The trickiest part of stranded knitting is maintaining an even
tension; the more sts you're carrying the yarn across in the back,
the more careful you have to be. It helps to space out the sts on the
needle a bit as you're carrying the yarn behind them.

Step 11: After completing the chart, knit one round with color A,
then work 3 rounds 1-inch x 1-inch ribbing. Bind off.

Step 12: For the cord, cut two pieces of color A and 1 piece of
color B about 5 feet long (or a bit more than twice the desired
cord length). Double each piece and braid the three doubled pieces
together. (If you prefer to make
an i-cord, by all means do that
instead.) Attach the ends of the
braid to opposite sides of the
cozy. Weave in all ends and enjoy!

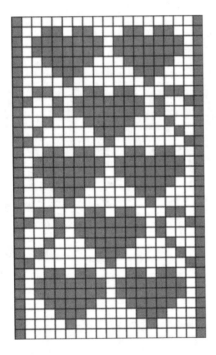

About the Designer:

Lucia Hicks is a part-time technical writer
and full-time primate rancher (a.k.a. mom)
who knits and spins whenever she can. She
would be quite willing to think inside the
box if she could ever find it. She blogs at
http://rhymeswithfuchsia.blogspot.com
about knitting, cats, and life in general.

Knitted Swiffer Cover

❀

A little household task takes on a craftified edge with some cotton yarn and a little creativity.

Gauge: 14 sts x 24 rows = 4" in ss

MATERIALS:

♦ **Yarn:** 1.25 oz kitchen cotton

Yarn needle to weave in ends

♦ **Needles:** Size 5.50 mm knitting needles

INSTRUCTIONS:

CO 43

Rows 1–3: K

Row 4: K

Row 5: K3, P37, K3

Rows 6–13: rep rows 4-5

Rows 14–31: K1, P1

Rows 32—39: rep Rows 4-5

Rows 40–43: K

BO, weave in ends.

Acknowledgments

Thank you to all of my friends and family who tolerate letting me telling their stories. My family has been most gracious of all with their tall tales and has listened to many of my own—thank you Dad, Laurie, Guy, and Eric. My dear friend Drew has not only given me years of funny content, he also helped create or arrange many of the patterns for this book, and for that, I am infinitely grateful.

The patterns came together with his help and that of other talented designers—Myra Wood, Marty Miller, Lucia Hicks, and Courtney Miller-Callihan, who is not just a fine knitter but also my agent. I prefer everyone in my life to be multipurpose. Courtney cranked out ten miles of i-cord and my contract all in the same month.

There's a whole team of people who go into making a book, and HCI isn't just my team; they feel like my extended family. Next time we all get together I expect there to be potato salad and cold drinks and someone falling into the pool. I'm grateful to Peter Vegso for signing the checks even when my proposal still had no title. Kim Weiss is my stellar publicist, but more importantly, she's my friend and my co-conspirator in self-help. Andrea Perrine Brower designed the fun cover and Jose Garcia and his team put the whole show online (special kudos Terry York!) Thanks to Lawna Oldfield for the fabulous photography as well as the layout and design. As always, I'm so appreciative of the sales folks for their support, and hats and shirts off to the hottest salesman in publishing, Sean Geary, who can talk anyone into anything.

None of those people would have ever laid hands on this book, though, if it weren't for my editor Allison Janse. She's read more about me and my life than any other human being on the planet and she still speaks to me. Without her, I would be nothing but comma splices and run-on sentences and long stories about my car. She's a talented editor and not a bad therapist, either. Allison, without you no one would be reading. You've changed my life forever. Thank you, and sorry about the drunken phone calls.

Finally, thank you to all my loyal readers online, especially the crazy cat ladies. And the dog ladies, too.

About the Author

Laurie Perry knits and writes in Los Angeles, California, where she chronicles her daily life on her online diary, Crazy Aunt Purl (www.crazyauntpurl.com). She has been featured in *Vogue Knitting* and *The Wall Street Journal,* and on MSN.com. She has written for the *Los Angeles Daily News* and the *Winter Haven News Chief* in Winter Haven, Florida. Her first book was *Drunk, Divorced, and Covered in Cat Hair.* Visit her at: www.crazyauntpurl.com.

More Crazy Aunt Purl...

Crazy Aunt Purl's
Drunk, Divorced & Covered in Cat Hair

The True-Life Misadventures of a 30-Something Who Learned to Knit After He Split

Laurie Perry aka Crazy Aunt Purl

Code # 5911 • Paperback • $15.95

Drunk, Divorced, and Covered in Cat Hair is the irreverent first-person narrative of a contemporary, displaced Southern woman facing life after her husband leaves her to "get his creativity back." Readers will laugh and cry with her as she gets dumped, makes new friends, gains weight (aka The Divorce Diet), travels abroad, and navigates the ins and outs of the modern dating scene. With her sense of humor and broken heart, she chronicles how "picking up sticks" helps her to pick up her life.

Hand Warmers

See instructions on page 154

1

Hand Warmers

See instructions on page 154

2

4

Lonely Hearts Personal Massager Cozy

See instructions on page 193

Flip-Flop Coaster

See instructions on page 189

5

Retro Toilet-Seat Cover

& Toilet-Paper Cozy

See instructions on page 184

Knitted
Swiffer Cover

See instructions on page 197

6

Mistake Rib Scarf

See instructions on page 157

Island Beach Bag

See instructions on page 172

7

Reversible
Halloweenie Beanie

See instructions on page 163

Pumpkin Beanie
with Curly Stem
or Pom-Pom

See instructions on page 165

8